being black

VIKING
COMPASS

being black

Zen and the Art of Living
with Fearlessness
and Grace

ANGEL KYODO WILLIAMS

VIKING COMPASS

VIKING COMPASS
Published by the Penguin Group
Penguin Putnam Inc., 375 Hudson Street,
New York, New York 10014, U.S.A.
Penguin Books Ltd, 27 Wrights Lane, London W8 5TZ, England
Penguin Books Australia Ltd, Ringwood, Victoria, Australia
Penguin Books Canada Ltd, 10 Alcorn Avenue,
Toronto, Ontario, Canada M4V 3B2
Penguin Books (N.Z.) Ltd, 182–190 Wairau Road,
Auckland 10, New Zealand

Penguin Books Ltd, Registered Offices:
Harmondsworth, Middlesex, England

First published in 2000 by Viking Compass,
a member of Penguin Putnam Inc.

1   3   5   7   9   10   8   6   4   2

Illustrations in Chapter Four by Deadra Bryant

LIBRARY OF CONGRESS CATALOGING-IN-PUBLICATION DATA
Williams, Angel Kyodo.
Being black : Zen and the art of living with fearlessness
and grace / Angel Kyodo Williams.
p. cm.
ISBN 0-670-89268-8
1. Spiritual life—Zen Buddhism. 2. Enlightenment
(Zen Buddhism) I. Title.
BQ9288.W54 2000
294.3'444—dc21   00-034964

This book is printed on acid-free paper.
∞

Printed in the United States of America
Set in Weiss
Designed by Francesca Belanger

For
my Grandfather
Clarence H. Williams,
my teacher
Sensei Pat Enkyo O'Hara,
and for my muse.

And to all those who have made
Being Awake a matter of
Life and Death

Your unfathomable excellence
pervades
everywhere.

Do not believe in anything simply because you have heard it. Do not believe in anything simply because it is spoken and rumored by many. Do not believe in anything simply because it is found written in your religious books. Do not believe in anything merely on the authority of your teachers and elders. Do not believe in traditions because they have been handed down for many generations. But after observation and analysis, when you find that anything agrees with reason and is conducive to the good and benefit of one and all, then accept it and live up to it.

—**Buddha**, The Enlightened One

ACKNOWLEDGMENTS

In Buddhist practice, the gentle placing of the two palms together signifies nonduality, unity. It is a bringing together of you and me, self and other, this and that; acknowledging all of it as One.

In Zen, it is called *gassho*.

This book is the result of an extraordinary amount of "this and that" coming together over the years. A multitude of experiences, conversations, images, relationships, musical notes, idle thoughts, and empty spaces are all here—each experience, every second as important as the last. I am equally grateful for the moments of pain that have made me so aware of the infinite bliss that is always just one moment away. So I acknowledge, in no particular order, some of those that have contributed to my life and hence this book, in so many ways.

To any one or any thing that is not mentioned here, it's only because I have been blessed by so many that my memory is not as great as the gifts.

First and always, to my mother and #1 fan, Mozella Gatewood, who gave me a reading bug with 400-page books at the age of nine. Yes, I thank you for correcting the manuscript when I couldn't stand to look at it anymore. But more important, I will always honor the gift of your tireless spirit, dramatic creativity, and boundless imagination, without which I never could have dreamed this book into reality. I especially thank you for not even being surprised.

To my father, Allen "Butch" Williams, my most sincere gratitude for making the choice to raise a girl child even when you wanted to go play stickball with the fellas because you were not much more than a boy yourself.

My cousins, Cindy Flowers, Tomeca, Robbie, and Jason, for being a family when I thought I was not ready, making me see that we never are and always are. My love to all of my family, who I know care whether they are able, in this moment, to be present or not, especially Berniece Gatewood, who gave me a home when I had none. Love to Delores, Beverly, Lynn, Marion, Hope Dawn, Sheryl, and all y'all's kids.

To my own family, Lexus and Legend, my rottweilers, who brought me years of joy, thank you for sharing your light and your lives with me.

To Eileen Cope, my perfect, incredible agent, for your unwavering support, careful shielding, and keen sensibility. There's nothing quite like being on the same page. My gratitude to you, Barbara, and the staff at Barbara Lowenstein Associates for making it all appear effortless.

To my gracious and intelligent editor, Janet Goldstein, whose patience with a sometimes resistant and always willful first-time writer has never gone unnoticed. Your contributions, suggestions, pushing, and prodding were all equally necessary and appreciated.

To my best friend and heart, Winston Francis, whom I never have to say much to. I love you, Winnie, and could not have chosen anyone better to continue to grow up with. Who'd've figured this is what we'd get from a Mr. Softee truck?

There are few that I grew with as much as my sister-friend Rebecca, who said that I could. Your generous sharing of time, space, and energy showed me that this was possible. Thank you, Lovey. As you have become like a sister to me, Alice has been like a second mother. Alice, you have always been most generous and sup-

Acknowledgments

portive; I remain humbled and speechless. And to Gloria and Amy, who *always* treat me like family and are also eternally supportive, great big warm hugs.

To my MoFo, Rene Cabrera, "Whassssssuuuup!" I will always seek you out for a latte and sesame bagel in a dank college town coffee shop when I am homesick. You are always close to my heart, Mr. Rene, and your presence and support will never be forgotten. I have you to thank in so many ways.

Though I have no idea where you are, my humble thanks to my freshman English professor at Nazareth College, Dr. Richard Loomis, who insisted with unabashed enthusiasm that I was a writer whether I cop to it, show up in class, or not. To my misplaced friend, Muna, who said that I should, I will always be deeply thankful for our inexplicable connection. To my "dharma brother" Jamie, whom I miss terribly, I know you are out there dancing beautifully somewhere.

My love to my sangha at the Village Zendo in New York City for making sure I always have a home to return to. Sybil Myoshin Taylor, writer, sister, friend, most amazing embodiment of courage and fearlessness, thank you for reminding me that I am not so crazy after all. To my dharma family—Bill, Jane, Julie, Julia, Mark, Wayne, Sinclair, Barbara, Daniel, both Susans, Tom, Tamaki, and to Neil—my humble thanks for sharing your expertise on my health without ever missing a beat. Peter, thank you for sharing your talent, wine, and Lisa's insight and excellent company on a moment's notice. Chris, I have no clue how you manage to trudge through my three-page-long e-mail and still smile over the telephone, always offering up wisdom served in a humble package. Deep *gassho* to Bernie Roshi and Jishu Sensei, cofounders of the Peacemaker Order, for not only their vision of peacemaking, but for the wisdom to empower others to extend that vision.

To His Holiness the Fourteenth Dalai Lama for his tireless and radical effort toward making Compassion the most-spoken language in the world.

Acknowledgments

Gratitude for my teachers, unbeknownst to them: Alice, Angela, bell, Bhimrao, Cornel, Ken, Mahatma, Malcolm, Martin, Pema, Shiko, Suzuki, Tenzin, Trungpa.

To my dear friends Hillary and Lorna for their interminable love, Brooklyn hideaway, and willingness to help me pick out clothes while listening to long-winded diatribes. Thanks to Greg Tate, ever the pusher and title approver, who not only recognizes but always points out the beauty of Being Black. Andy, my thanks for sanctuary when I most needed it and making me see the Zen of South Park, for you, I "Blame Canada." Arisa, you are my sunshine; Suhir, my partner in crime. To Renee for healing the healer, Taming the Shrew, and being *so* incredibly human.

Cree Bear, when you are able to read this, which I'm sure will be any moment now, know that it is your friendship and your smile that are most amazing to me, my littlest friend. Thank you for allowing me in your life. Certainly not last, to Cree's mommy, Gina, who knows deeply that we all just need to be heard—and so you listen.

Mmmmhmmmm . . . Heaven on Earth starts with Jamaica Blue with half and half and fresh ground nutmeg. Even when you thought you didn't know, you sang my Freedom Suite.

Yes, I feel the spirits and know that God is Love.

Love and life are inexhaustible.

Gassho to you all,

angel

CONTENTS

Contents

being black

Introduction

Black folks have arrived. Thirty-five years after Martin Luther King, Jr. articulated a dream of an America that would see the fall of the wall that so severely divides us as races, we have come to hold a definitive place in the politics, economics, and culture of our country.

We have made contributions of enormous proportion in every area of society without limitation. Our stories and vision are woven into the fabric of the American Dream. We play an increasingly significant part in and sometimes even dominate business, academics, sports, arts, music, and even that most powerful tool, language, in not just America, but the world community. And while we haven't yet been privy to the unqualified equal access that we are entitled to, we have made it clear to all who are watching that we have the breadth and diversity to penetrate and inform every area of society from aeronautics to zoology. We have essentially said to America, "You may have been resistant to letting us in, but we are here. We have crossed the threshold and can no longer be ignored or turned away."

And there's another side to our continuing story of success. Along with political, economic, and cultural growth, we are taking a new look at our individual growth and sense of who we are and who we can be in the world. At a time when many of us are no longer plagued by just how we can survive and live, we can begin to ask how we can live *better*. The questions of who we are and what role we play as black people in America now have room to coexist with the larger questions, "Who am I, and what role do I play as an individual in the world?" We want to know how we can be better mothers to our children, brothers to our sisters and lovers to our partners. Some of us ask how we can best give back or contribute to the community that has nurtured us as well as it could and is itself in continued need of nurturing.

For much of our history, the black Christian and Baptist church has been greatly instrumental in helping us to navigate these soul-searching questions. And for so many of us, the church still provides space to retreat from the world long enough to regroup and process what our collective life is about. But just as we are widely diverse as a people, with a range of interests and experiences, our spiritual needs have also branched out and diversified. We now have the ability and, more important, the sense of entitlement, to explore beyond our own immediate traditions and look at what the world has to offer us to help resolve these questions that are critical to our spirits.

The West in general, and America in particular, have spent the last fifty years developing an affinity for and relationship with Eastern philosophies that address body, mind and spirit. In sometimes sharp contrast to the West's bold, pressing progress in technology and other sciences, the East has fostered a sensibility of immeasurable depth, and a reverence for wisdom that transcends the knowledge that can be found on the pages of a book or developed in a lab. As a country and as a people, we are coming to terms with the fact that oftentimes the race for outward material achievement is run at the expense of our inner sense of spirit and connectedness with our world, and even with our own individual lives.

While we don't necessarily have to be looking to replace our traditional religions, we can appreciate the benefit of weaving some of the very useful practices and ideals of ancient Eastern wisdom into our daily lives. Just as we have recollected the valuable aspects of the African-derived belief systems of Yoruba, Santería, and even Voodoo, many of us have also taken the liberty of exploring Islam, Hinduism, Sufism, or one of the different schools of Buddhism. We have seized the opportunity to incorporate such practices as honoring our ancestors, creating sacred spaces, and bowing down in thanks to the gifts that nature brings into our lives.

On the other hand, some of us are not even looking . . . or at least we haven't known it. Early in my life, like many young black children, I went to a Baptist church on Sundays with the woman who took care of me and doubled as my father's girlfriend after my parents separated. My dad was raised Catholic but was never a churchgoer himself, so I was the one that got to sing in the hand-clapping, foot-stomping choir with a paper doily pinned to my head, and who looked on in wondrous amazement at the women and men that "caught the Holy Ghost." They shimmy-shook their way down the aisle to the pastor to get a witness to the touching of their soul by a God and His Son that I didn't quite understand and never got a chance to see.

At eight, I got a new stepmother and a new church. The more reserved nature of the Protestant church, with its studious Sunday schools and engaging activities like Christmas plays and basketball, appealed to my mind. I became an admitted fan of the long-haired, blue-eyed Jesus I saw pictured in the heavy, all-white King James version of the Bible that my stepmother kept. I felt a connection to both the compassion that He must have felt to allow himself to be sacrificed for us, and to the depth of pain

He suffered as He sought insight into His father's wisdom with the haunting query, "My Lord, my Lord, why hast thou forsaken me?" Still, by the time I was twelve, I declared myself an agnostic. I stopped going to church and fell out of sync with a lot of the people around me. As I got older, I noticed other ways in which I didn't quite fit in.

I didn't believe I had any sense of style or aesthetic because none of the art or design of things around me appealed to me. That all changed when I saw a traditional Japanese house and garden for the first time. I discovered that I didn't lack a sense of home, it was just that my sensibility was more attuned to the Eastern hemisphere than to the Western one. To put it simply, the clean, open space spoke to me and I could see how it could work for me without having to be filled up with things. Empty was no longer empty. After that encounter with "home," I began to see things with different eyes. It was as if I had been blind to the beauty of things and now I could see. It sounds silly now, but because I thought it was Japanese culture that I had found an affinity with, I ran off looking for any book I could find with the words "Japanese Culture" in it.

What I found was a classic Zen book called, what else, *Zen and Japanese Culture*, by a scholar named D. T. Suzuki who happened to also study Zen. He wasn't a priest or monk, but like many other people, he practiced Zen as a lay person. No robes, no titles, just an appreciation for a method of training that seemed to have the trappings of a religion, but at its foundation held something more, something profound. Being a scholar, Suzuki wrote about it. His writing did a lot to bring Zen to the West and to America, but I didn't know that then. All I knew was that it wasn't Japanese culture that I was having a love affair with . . . it was the culture and sensibility that came from Zen.

Most of us think of Buddhism as one big religion or philosophy with a fixed set of beliefs, views, and practices. Sometimes that confusion comes from the way people talk about it. They say "Buddhists believe such and such" or "In Buddhism, they practice (blah, blah, blah)." People always ask me, "So you chant '*Namoo myo something, something,*' right?" They've no doubt seen Angela Bassett as Tina Turner in the movie *What's Love Got to Do with It?* (For the record: Everything.)

There is no doubt in my mind that Buddhism is a religion. It has rituals, traditions, schools, and hierarchical structures. However, Buddhist *philosophy*, in its purest form, is just a set of principles to help you become awake to the life that you have so that you can live it more completely. If we go back to the original ideas and strip away the extras, if we take the "ism" out of what a brother named Buddha taught, then it's no more and no less than a way of planning your life. It's setting up your social structures and actively engaging your time on this planet by waking up and getting a fundamental grasp on what's really important.

With a little awareness of who we are and our shared humanity with others, we can begin to relax a little. It doesn't mean we drop our battles, say "racism and violence don't exist anymore," or lose our passion to push for the rights and space that we should have as human beings. Maybe, though, we can begin to approach those efforts more as the work that is here for us to do, like washing those dishes in our house after someone else ate off them, rather than as a struggle, which makes us feel constrained as soon as we hear it. We set ourselves up for an "Us vs. Them" mentality, which is dangerous and, in all honesty, unrealistic. Wherever we are is Our House, and we must all live in this house together.

Lessons and insights we can learn from Buddhism can be applied to our lives this very minute. No matter what your situation or station in life, no matter what the color of your skin or the obstacles you face, you can create a better life right now. Even in Buddhist countries around the world that is the main goal of everyday people. While the people of Tibet appreciate the effort of the monks toward attaining spiritual enlightenment in this lifetime, their day-to-day reality is that they want prosperity and peace in their lives. Not such a bad set of desires, given that we each have a set. Each of us wants basically the same things.

People of color are especially in need of new ways and new answers to the separation and fear we face each day. It wouldn't be a stretch to say that as black people, more than most groups in this country, we live our daily lives with the distinct taste of fear in our mouths. We have lived with it and incorporated it into the fabric of our being, so much so that on the surface we may not even be aware of it anymore. But the fear is there and it permeates every aspect of our lives. Proving we are not afraid. Insisting we are not so different. Or acknowledging that we are different and should be accepted that way. Sometimes, in an effort to attain equal footing, we forget what is most important for us to tend to: our hearts, our spirits, going home to family and friends.

We need a way to rise up and peek out from under the smothering blankets and stigma of racism, classism, and out-of-control individualism. But we also need a way to put into perspective our fundamental sense of separation and confusion. Our rage, our love, our dreams and disappointments, the death of our loved ones, the blissful joys as well as the cruel facts of life. It's not the way of white folks we need to get a grasp on, it's the way of life.

The Zen principles offered here can provide a framework for creating the meaningful life we want to live, without dogma and restrictions. They can give us direction for addressing our innermost spiritual questions and experiencing their relevance to our lives.

While they are not an antidote to the underlying reasons for our fears, they can give us a different way to approach those fears. They can give us insight into the nature of all of our feelings—good, bad and indifferent—thus changing the way we receive each experience and live each moment. They absolutely can help us see ourselves as inseparable from others and inseparable from the happiness and healing of others.

Really, the simple ideas and practices are about our daily lives, and they wouldn't be of much use if they weren't. We are a practical folk, aren't we? What we really need to address is the baby crying in the other room, the train fare we have to scrape together, the deadline that we need to meet, and that girl that sits in the next cubicle and works our last nerve. In short, we want to know how to be here in this life and be okay just as we are. Like sculptors, we want to take this messy lump of clay that someone told us is our life and make a masterpiece of it . . . no matter what we've been told about who we are and what we can or cannot become. I have discovered that there really is an art to being here in this world and, like any other art, it can be mastered.

Even when we do recognize that we would like to be part of some larger change in our community, we sometimes have the tendency to feel that we have to wait. We think we need to be "perfect" as individuals in order to begin the work of contributing to our collective benefit. Before she passed away, Sandra Jishu Holmes, cofounder of the Peacemaker Community and a well-loved Zen teacher, wrote in her journal, "Only the wounded healer is able to heal. As long as we think that spiritual leaders need to be perfect, we live in poverty. I have a perfect teacher inside; there is no perfect teacher outside."

I originally came to write this book from a place of pain because, like so many of us, I have been wounded and still share space with that pain. I believe, as Jishu wrote, that sometimes it is necessary to know pain, to be intimate with it, to help others to heal. In the course of my practice, my biggest lesson has been how to open my heart and be aware of how I am feeling. I have learned to allow my pain to be what it is, honor it, and be gentle with myself and whatever faults I perceive. From that place, my world—my capacity for compassion, gentleness and clarity—has opened itself up before me. I now embrace my heart that hurts because it is the very same heart that heals. I think our communities can benefit from this lesson.

Spirit refers to that which gives life. The study of spirit, *spirituality*, is concerned with the essence of what gives life meaning, what makes it worth living. We must develop our appreciation of the human spirit. Spirituality, which takes a step beyond the limitations of our senses and makes a practice of honoring that spirit, may be the only path we can take to lead us to the freedom that we are so desperately looking for. If we had to choose one ideal, it is Love and the true practice of compassion that is the only political, religious, social construct or modality that we need to see ourselves through. With it firm in our hearts, we *can* see the dream of a King become a reality.

My own great discovery about Buddhism, Zen, and meditation practice as a whole is that there really isn't anything very special about it at all. The longer you look for something "special" that is beyond yourself and the tools that you already have available to you, the less likely you'll be to find what is there.

You, just as you are, and your life right here and right now, are all there is and all you need to know. You don't have to do anything special. Mostly, you have to be open to meeting face-to-face, and even dancing with, the truth that pertains to your life right now. You have to find a way to collect your fractured pieces, examine them and then accept them as part of who you are. Spiritual practice is about transformation, but it's also, and more important, about working with what is. All of us must learn to honor our whole selves just as we come, just as we are. We can do this by just living, just doing, just Being Black.

Part 1

the
nature of
our
existence

$$1$$

Four Simple
Truths

Wouldn't it be nice if someone offered you a map to navigate and negotiate your life by? It wouldn't be a complex city-type map, with so many signs and symbols that you don't know which way to go. Instead, this life map would be simple and clear, more like a treasure map. The map would have a very neat circle representing a specific destination, a place to arrive where you could rest and feel content, at ease.

Obviously, if there is a destination to which you can go indicated on your map, there would also be a path to get there. It would be bold and clear, and would stand out from all its surroundings.

If you traced your finger backward along the line, the map would have a thick red **X** to show you the starting point. That way, no matter where you were in life, if you felt lost, you would only have to look at the big **X** to gain perspective on how to continue on your journey.

Finally, like all good maps, this life map would have a key. The key would be your reference point for understanding the map. It would be the foundation on which the map was built. If you studied the whole map for a while, you could put it down and probably still remember the important things when you really needed to.

What if you paid extra-special attention to the map, gave it your full concentration, until you knew it by heart? No doubt you would be able to approach the task of making your way through life with a deeper understanding of the bumps, curves, mountains, and valleys that you are sure to encounter every day.

In many ways, we are like noble warriors that have somehow been separated from our tribe or clan. We are out in the woods lost and alone, without a map to guide us back. We have forgotten how to use the skills that are the marks of true warriors. In our hearts, we know that we have something great, even beautiful, to accomplish while we are here. We know that we have a grandness and elegance inside us, and we really want to live up to it. But without our skills, we feel stuck and cannot move forward. We know, very deep down, that we do have the ability to manage any situation that comes to us. But because we have lost touch with our true nature and awareness of our abilities, we remain in fear.

It is only natural that as human beings we want to feel happy, satisfied, and secure. But early on, we are given messages that attack our sense of ease with who we are. We are not bright enough, or tall enough. As black people, we learn that our skin color is not right, our hair too kinky or curly, our lips too full and our presence too strong. Sometimes these messages are subtle, and at other times they are harshly direct. We carry all of these lessons inside us everywhere we go. They become the box from which we operate and see ourselves. Inside this box, we become smaller and smaller, and forget how amazing we really are.

Because it seems way too hard to confront, and because we were never taught differently, we put many of these feelings in our back pockets. Our coping mechanism of choice is to ignore. To say "'sall good" or "That's alright . . . whatever," when really we do not feel alright. We learn to turn and look the other direction whenever something uncomfortable or negative comes our way. As a result we live with these small, nagging sensations of inner dissatisfaction and inadequacy without rest. This internal discomfort plagues us on a daily basis. From time to time it reveals itself as a questioning of the meaning of our lives. We want to know why we cannot be happier than we are, feel better than we feel, get more of what we want, and enjoy life more than we do.

On the surface, in full view of the world, we are working our jobs and paying our bills (or trying to, anyway). We are trying hard to manage our existence. But many of us feel lost, out of place. We describe this feeling in many ways. We say, "I don't know, I'm just not happy." "I know I should be doing something more with my life." "I feel as if I haven't found my purpose." Often we are not only unable to express how we feel, we do not even know what these feelings are about. Instead, we just feel ill at ease and move through our lives with a sense of agitation and irritability. We may even treat other people with disregard because we don't know how else to express our inner dissatisfaction.

This feeling of being out of place is particularly disturbing to us because we usually feel as if we are experiencing it alone. Everyone else seems to belong to this life, to this universe, more than we do. We feel powerless because we believe we do not have the skills we need to master our lives.

Life is truly an art form. It is like any art form—painting, sculpting, playing an instrument or a sport—in that you have to develop your skills in order to be masterful. Even though you may not think of it this way, no matter how excellent you get at whatever your art is, you started out with the basic ingredients for that skillfulness right from the beginning. When we watch Michael Jordan soar high above the rim, hear a Miles Davis riff, or look at a Jean-Michel Basquiat painting, it seems amazing that they could be so good at their arts. It's as if they were just born that way. And it's true, they were. So were you and I.

We have all the basic skills we need to master the art that we call life. But usually, we forget this. Either we are not reminded of it enough or we were simply never told. So we go around in life feeling as if we don't really know what we are doing. Or we spend a lot of time pretending that we're in control when deep down, we feel exactly the opposite. Either way, we end up wishing someone would give us a cheat-sheet that we could use to find a quick fix to everything that bothers us. We want to know how we can just get everything right, *fast.*

There are lots of things I don't know, but the one thing I know for sure is that there is no quick fix for our lives. The first reason that the quick fix doesn't exist is because nothing truly valuable happens quickly. Every art requires practice, even if you are a natural. Michael lived in his backyard basketball court. Miles played relentlessly and constantly. Basquiat studied the masters.

The second and more important reason that we never find a quick fix is because we don't need it. There *is* nothing to fix. We already have the skills we need to accomplish everything we truly want, to access everything we really need. The only thing we have to do is to see that the skills are present in ourselves and then sharpen them up with practice so we can use them effortlessly.

The closest thing we can get to a cheat-sheet might be some guidelines and pointers that help us look in the right direction. So a map, with a key, would be very helpful. In fact, such a map is available for us already.

Some 2,500 years ago, a warrior-prince who felt the same sense of unease left his comfortable, wealthy life, his palace and his clan behind him. He set out on a journey searching for the essential truth about life. He wanted to know why old age, sickness, and death existed; why life seemed plagued with misery. After a lot of effort, this prince who would become known as the Buddha, meaning "the awakened one" or "one that has been enlightened," saw clearly the truth about life. From that point on, he made it his life's work to create a map that others could use.

He broke his directions down to Four Simple Truths that go something like this:

1. Life is uncomfortable.

At first, this simple truth seems *so* simple that there is no revelation in it at all. And really, that is exactly the case. As a part of our ongoing life experience, we are prone to discomfort.

There are the mundane, everyday discomforts: *This apartment is too hot. Outside is too cold. The train is too crowded. My parents make me crazy. My kids are too grown. My lover is cheating. I hate my job, I hate my boss, I hate doing dishes, and will somebody* please *turn that hip-hop off!* There is a constant stream of small distractions that plague us like flies buzzing in our ears.

Physical pain is part of this discomfort as well. The aches and pains of our own bodies come from many different sources. When we are not careful, we cut ourselves with a knife or the edge of a piece of paper. We lift something that is too heavy and our backs suffer. We overdo it at the gym and end up sore the next day. As we get older, parts of our body that were unprovoked begin to nag at us. Our knees get stiff and we can't get up as fast as we used to. Older still, our bodies begin to seem no longer our own. We cannot walk as fast or run as far. Stairs suddenly seem twice as long. As with any complex machinery, especially if we have not taken good care of our bodies, or have just outright abused them, they will begin to fail us.

There are also the discomforts of illness and disease. We may suffer from stress and get ulcers. We may abuse alcohol or drugs that damage our bodies inside and out. Our lungs may become blackened from excess cigarettes, cigars, or marijuana. And while the rest of the country is becoming more educated about AIDS, black people—and black women in particular—have the fastest growing number of cases. We lose our minds to Alzheimer's and our bodies to cancers. Suffering and discomfort seem to be everywhere and without end.

If that isn't enough, our lives are punctuated by crises that cause us pain. We lose the job we thought we hated but now, unemployed, our dilemma is greater than before. The predicament of a cousin in jail or a sister fleeing an abusive partner brings home to us how profoundly we can all be affected by family turmoil. As so many of us know firsthand, heartbreak can feel just like it sounds, bringing with it large doses of pain that are not always easy to let go of. Finally, there are the deaths of our loved ones, bringing with them grief and sadness that seem too much to bear.

More so than our daily discomforts, the pain of tragic, abrupt or otherwise upsetting events in our lives serve as sharp reminders that life is not within our control. We feel shuffled around by it, cast this way and that with nothing to hold on to. There seems to be no end to the potential for discomfort and pain, and we live our lives in fear of meeting them again. We become intimate with pain and discomfort very early in life. From our earliest lessons that not everything is within our control, to this very moment, most of us are in a neverending battle with our own discomfort.

So life *is* uncomfortable, that much is true. But we knew this already, didn't we? Even if we have not said it in such simple terms.

We may feel a moment of relief at having it revealed in such a clear way: *It is not just me. I am not crazy, nor am I alone.* The truth is that life is *full* of suffering and pain. Everywhere you look, whether you turn on the television or walk outside your own door, once you are aware of this truth, you notice it more readily. Look! There is pain. There is pain among people of all ages, races, incomes, and education levels. We are all experiencing discomfort. We are all suffering.

Once you know this simple truth in your heart, it becomes the key to understanding the nature of your own existence. It may not happen in this very second, or tomorrow, or next week, but some experience or feeling at some time will bring this simple truth home to you. It will not be words in a book or a passing thought; you will feel it. It will open up before you and be as clear as the bright blue sky on the most perfect day. In that moment, the First Simple Truth that life *is* uncomfortable will be profound.

2. Desire causes discomfort.

As humans, we are in a constant state of suffering over who we are and our life situation. By this, I mean that we feel that we are poor when it comes to what we have in our package to present to the world. We never feel that we have enough. We always want more of this or extra that. *If I had that coat, I would be so happy. If I could just get this job or meet the right person, everything would change and my life would be better.* Of course, when you get the coat or the job or the new lover, there is another someone or something that comes along in a few days or months or years that seems better, brighter, and more appealing.

We do this in all areas of our lives, from the smallest to the greatest. It is this wanting, this ever-present, unchecked desire that is at the root of our discomfort. We possess a constant craving and insistent desire for things to be either different than they are or to stay the way we want them to be longer. We develop fixed ideas about the way things should be and the ways we always imagine things should be different. We think we should have a bigger car or get with that person (or situation). If you tell yourself often enough that this is the way it should be, you begin to believe that idea in your mind, no matter where the idea came from to begin with.

As human beings, we have a habit of attaching ourselves to things, people, and situations, and holding on tight. In turn, that clinging becomes the single source of our conflict, tension, and frustration. Why? Because we really can't control all of the elements that go into making up life. And because we are human, we are self-centered, so it is heartbreaking to realize that things do not necessarily go our way and we are not the center of the universe.

Some days it seems like the world has it in for us, trying to ruin our days or plans in a series of bad events stacked up one after the other. But life really has no interest in whether we want it to turn left or turn right. It is only the fact that we view our own desires as special that makes us think we should have things exactly as we want them. Our desires must be more special than anyone else's. It may be perfect in our minds that the grocery store is open on a holiday because we forgot to get bread. But the cashier is miserable because he wanted to go to the movies instead of working. Had he not come to work, he may have lost his job. In that moment you are happy and he is not. But we are only concerned with the benefits that *we* get from each situation. That is what I mean when I say that we are self-centered.

Our wanting and desires are often in direct conflict with the reality of the current moment. No matter how much we want it to be dry and sunny because we have plans for our day, the fact is that it is raining. There is nothing we can do about it. So we sulk and curse and complain. *If it hadn't rained, I could have done my laundry or gone to the park. Why did it have to rain today? How inconvenient this is for me.* Nature goes about its business despite our plans and it continues to rain. We are inside, miserable and discontented. We can become intensely self-centered in these moments.

Sometimes, our wanting seems grand and altruistic, and we do not think of it as something that we cling to. *All I want is to be a better person. I would become more spiritual if I went to temple (or church or the mosque) more often. I will speak quietly and keep my eyes cast to the floor. I will become a reverend, a priestess, or a nun. I'll be the perfect father. I'll be a Super Wife.* Secretly, we may begin to think of the result. *If I do these things, I will be better than these people around me. They will see me as special and I will be revered.* We shouldn't fool ourselves, because before we know it, such a goal can become one and the same as wanting and desire.

In communities of color, we have lived for a long time without access to the material possessions that signify success in our country. We know that we are just as worthy, and we desperately want to have a measure of our equality with white people. This has contributed to a rampant, crippling case of a need for instant gratification. This may be the cornerstone of American culture in general, but it seems to be in overdrive where black folks are concerned, where there's an entrenched belief that who you are is directly related to what you have.

When persistent craving is combined with a need for instant gratification, the possibility for discomfort is doubled. If desire sends us on a journey toward accumulation, instant gratification propels us at light speed. By giving in to this need, we rob ourselves of thoughtful decision-making. We are more likely to spend recklessly. We do not save. We are even less realistic about what we actually need. The desire for instant gratification is at the heart of substance abuse. We want to "feel good," so we drink, or we smoke, or do anything to get a high. Soon we are unable *not* to want it, and an addiction is born.

Our teenagers see their peers—white, black, and otherwise—with the latest jeans, video game, or sneakers. They have been taught that they need status symbols to maintain a strong appearance, to be important. Aggression and violence are fueled by the sense that we should have what we want immediately and without regard or respect for anyone that gets in the way. If someone else has it and I want it now, why shouldn't I take it from them?

We compete amongst ourselves for ownership of the title of "Having the Most" or "Looking the Best." Instant gratification promotes divisiveness amongst our children and ourselves. As a group, we have become easy targets for advertising and marketing. Contrary to popular opinion, the black consumer market is the most brand-conscious. We are easily sold on alcohol and cigarettes. We spend more of our income on commercial products than any other group in this country. If you can brand it, you can be sure that black people will buy it.

There are many cases in which we have to work harder than someone else to reach the same goal. This makes it even more urgent that we make an effort to be aware of how our desires operate in our lives. We can become so full of the *sense* of wanting, that we do not take the time to *feel* whether we really want or not. We do not know where wanting ends and where we begin.

We become very accustomed to giving unnecessary attention to each and every thing that does not suit us. We spend a lot of time wanting, wanting, wanting, and even when we get what we want, we find ways to be dissatisfied. We fret that something is not just the way we want it, how we want it, when we want it.

Soon, what starts out as just our personal preference can take over and become the perspective from which we see our lives, and even the lives of other people. Eventually, less and less of the way things are is satisfactory to us. Given the fact that we don't have control over every aspect of life, it is not just our desires that cause us discomfort, but the sense that we are most important. The idea of me and mine, separate from everything else, is what creates a sense of craving.

When we finally recognize our desires, and the way in which we attach ourselves to them, as the root of our discomfort, we gain a reference point for ending our pain. When we are feeling pain, we can remind ourselves that some desire or another is the source of it. Knowing this alone doesn't make the pain go away, but it does help. For most of us, the not-knowing makes us even more uncomfortable.

With desires and cravings as persistent and pervasive as they are, we may be tempted to give in to the idea that this is just the way it is. Obviously there's no way *around* discomfort, which is tucked into too many places in our lives. But it *is* possible to move beyond it.

3. It is possible to end discomfort.

If we aren't supposed to want anything, you may be wondering, is the solution to discard all of our possessions, be naked and live off the land? Should we really only eat and drink what is absolutely necessary to sustain our lives? And what about love and happiness? Should we stop wanting joy and pleasure in our lives?

The answer to all of these questions, thankfully, is a loud NO.

It is basic to all beings to want to achieve happiness. Not only is it basic to our nature, it is our fundamental right. We not only want happiness, but we should have the freedom to be able to pursue it to the fullest of our capacity. We all want to experience life in a way that makes us feel complete and connected to all that is good.

The Third Simple Truth is very easy and a logical conclusion to come to. Once we have discovered that our wanting is the source of our discomfort, it makes sense that if we could eliminate or, at the very least, reduce the wanting, the discomfort would go right out the door with it. Reducing our desires and eliminating false neediness is the answer to resolving the nagging inner discomfort that we feel.

Yet if it is *me* that is wanting, how is it possible to rid myself of unnecessary wanting without getting rid of me?

Many people mistakenly believe that the way to be spiritual and find peace in their lives is to wrestle the "me" to the ground. To conquer it. To force themselves to submit to a set of ideas about how they should be. They begin a process of tightening themselves, cutting off their feelings or pretending not to see, in order to reach their goal. "I am not angry," they tell themselves. "I will stop drinking alcohol right now and never drink it again." "I will not do anything wrong, ever."

This doesn't work. Instead, this new desire to achieve a goal takes over and it is just another desire. We can't simply look in the mirror and say we want to be better and believe that such thoughts will make it so. The wanting takes over again. Wanting is wanting is wanting. What we are looking for is not-wanting.

If we release our fixed ideas about how the world should appear, desires can simply fall away. Our attention is paid to releasing, not wanting to release. We have heard this called "letting go." Once we let go of our desires, we find that a calmer, more graceful way of existing is revealed. It has been there all along, but the wanting has made it difficult to recognize.

So the question is, How can we release our wanting, and with it our discomfort, without creating another problem at the same time?

4. Meditation and the eightfold path can end discomfort.

When the Buddha went out on his journey to find the answer to life, he didn't hit on it right away. He followed a lot of different teachers and took up different practices. For a while, he even became fanatical and was very harsh with himself and his body. But he soon realized that this was not the way to go either.

In the end, he simply sat down and paid attention to the way in which his mind worked. What he saw was how busy his thoughts were and how difficult they were to control. After a while, he stopped trying to control them. With practice, his mind became quiet. With his mind quiet, the Buddha could finally see that so much of what we react to in the world is just something we have made up in our minds. It was there, in the stillness of his mind, that he found the way to eliminate discomfort. If we didn't spend so much time reacting to things, we would spend less time feeling bothered. We would be able to relax in our lives the way our mind relaxes in meditation.

Meditation (discussed fully in Chapter 7) is one of eight steps that we can follow to reduce the troubling sense of unease that we live with. What we will find when discomfort is reduced is that we can be in the world in a way that is less difficult and distracting. We can see the world in a way that allows us to open our hearts to everyone else in it. When we begin to understand the nature of everything, our vision of ourselves and our lives expands.

These Four Simple Truths are the key, starting point, path, and destination on our map to negotiate life by. If we purposely or lazily ignore the fact that we have a map, we are more likely to remain lost.

These truths, and the idea of enlightened being have nothing to do with any religion. They are universal and belong to all of us. Being human, with all our flaws, faults, and broken parts, is a unique and precious gift. We have been blessed with consciousness of our actions, and with that, the ability to change them.

2

Three Wonderful
Treasures

As simple as the truths may be, it can seem like an overwhelming task to try to shift the way we usually are in the world so that we can be more at ease in it. After all, you have been You your whole life! Every year, every month, every day and second of your life has shaped the person you are right now.

How can we possibly begin to change? Because we are so used to being who we are, it seems foreign even to think that we can change. We usually have a fixed set of ideas about who we are: *I'm a nice person usually, but I get real mean if I don't get enough sleep. I've just always been this way.* Or *I really like buying expensive clothes and shoes. Sometimes I don't really have the money for it, but I do what I have to do to get them because that's just the way I am.* We say that a lot. *That's just the way I am. That's just the way he is or she is.* It's as if we think we came out of the womb already knowing what Tommy Hilfiger, Nike, and the Gap are, and that we like them.

We Are Always Changing

The truth is that the way we perceive who we are has much more to do with our experiences than with a certain set of traits that we are given at birth. However, while we realize that we can change our hair color or style, and dress up in a slick suit or down in a pair of old sweats, most of us don't think it's possible to change anything about who we "really" are. Aside from mostly physical genetic things, the so-called "who we are" is capable of amazing change. In fact, change happens whether we want it to or not. We have always been changing and are always different in some ways than we were before. We know that we are definitely not the six-year-olds that panicked about being left alone on our first days of school. And thank goodness we're not the goofy-toothed, big hair-having, too-red-lipstick-wearing, anxiety-ridden teens in our high school yearbooks anymore. We recognize ourselves visually, but we are very clear that inside, we don't think or feel the same as those memories on the page. Seeing how much we have changed already in this life, why would we think that we cannot continue to do so? And if we know change is going to happen in our life anyway, why not be active participants whenever we can?

Maybe the more important question is, Do we really want to change? Will it take away from who we are, make us feel less alive, less cool, less sexy or less fine? We think about who we are and decide that "we're not so bad," so maybe we don't really want to change. Again, this has to do with the fact that we think of ourselves as fixed, we're just "this way."

The resistance to change comes from a fear deep inside of us that says *Maybe if I change, I won't recognize myself.* There are things we really like about who we are and we don't want to lose them. Personally, I don't feel as if I'm so bad that I need to trade in everything about the way I am in exchange for being more real and happier in my life. This is very important: Making changes in the way that you see and handle life is not about giving up who you are. It's not about forcefully giving up anything at all. It's not like quitting cigarettes or chocolate. Let's face it, even though we really want to feel better in our lives and be more spiritually connected, most of us are not going to give away all of our worldly possessions and go live in some cave on a snowy mountaintop. And the beauty of it is that we don't have to. That may work for one or two of us out of thousands, but it's important that us "real world" people feel like we can take simple steps to help us master life more easily *without* having to give up our present lives.

If being more spiritual, more aware in your own life means completely giving up the life you have, why would anyone bother to trade? We don't want to toss away the life we have. We want both to keep our lives and our personal style *and* be more content in them. The idea is not to throw away what you have, but to make what you have easier to use.

Signing Up for Enlightenment

My own interest in Zen made me find my way to an American Zen monastery. I had become intensely interested in Buddhism and wanted to absorb as much of it as I could. For a couple of years, I had been checking out different meditation centers in both San Francisco and New York, and made a point of finding one wherever I went. I got a lot out of going to the centers but still felt that I wanted to have a more "complete" experience. There was something stirring deep in me and I knew I was getting pretty serious about making the practice of Zen a much larger part of my life. But I still needed to assure myself that I knew what I was getting into. I knew about a monastery right outside New York City that I could go to to get the whole experience. It seemed like just the thing I needed to feed my appetite for more.

I signed up for a weekend retreat, packed my bag, and got on the bus. Of course I felt completely foreign when I got there. Not only was I the only black person (there were two Asian women), but quite a few of the other people were fully dressed in monks' gear. They looked like they could have stepped right out of a samurai movie, shaved heads and all. At the centers that I had gone to, some people had worn robes while doing their meditation practice, and the teachers always had the whole outfit on, but this was different. These were not mysterious Tibetan or Japanese monks looking foreign and exotic. They were plain old Americans, just like men and women that you had seen on the street earlier that day. The monks were like a band of black-clad angels that seemed to float past everyone with no effort. They did a whole routine of checking people in, assigning rooms, making introductions, and overseeing a big group meal without ever seeming disturbed by anything.

In the early morning (at the outrageous hour of 4:30 A.M.) the monks prepared the big hall for meditation, woke everyone up, and conducted an elaborate ceremony of bells being rung, gongs being gonged, and 60 people chanting in unison. Then they hustled us off to breakfast. All of this was done by 8 A.M. They did it all while wisping by in their flowing robes without ever saying a word. I fell in love! I decided right then that what I wanted was to become a monk. What better way was there to advance very quickly than to live this way, taking care of the monastery, studying, practicing all the time? I thought it would be the perfect opportunity to get away from the daily distractions that were keeping me from really seeing life clearly. I could concentrate only on Zen and have nothing else to disturb me.

I went to the teacher and told him how convinced I was that

I wanted to be a monk. He listened intently and then asked me questions to probe how serious I was. I left the interview feeling confident that I had just taken a big step toward being a much better person. The next day, the teacher talked about monks and how they led a life of service to the community. Monks, he said, were "home-leavers." They were dependent on the community to support them because they had left home and given up everything they'd possessed in order to serve. In fact, he said, it was *essential* for them to leave their homes behind and not have responsibilities to anything else.

I was confused. Home-leavers? As in leave home? I couldn't do this. I couldn't leave my home. I could leave my job in a hot minute, but at home I had a life that I felt I couldn't walk away from no matter how much I wanted to study Zen. After I returned home, I thought about it and talked about it a lot for the next few months. My partner was very understanding, considering that I was basically looking for some kind of permission to leave and go live up on a hill with some robes and no money so I could be "more spiritual." I thought about it over and over again. The funny thing is that what really made me give up the idea was my dogs. I had two, and unlike the people that I would leave behind, my dogs depended on my being there for them. They couldn't just say, "Fine, go on with your spiritual journey . . . we'll be here when you get back." No, no one else would take care of two big Rottweilers for an unspecified amount of time. I wouldn't want anyone to and I couldn't possibly give them away. They were like my own children.

At first I was very disappointed at having to make this choice. I thought it said something about me. I thought it meant that I did not really have what it takes to be better, that I wasn't willing to sacrifice everything for my practice. I thought I would never get the hang of being more spiritual the way I was going. But after a while, little by little, I realized that the idea that you had to leave home in order to engage your life didn't make sense. Spirituality and responsible living are not objects that can be found somewhere outside of yourself. They are not at a monastery and they definitely don't wear robes. You can't catch enlightenment like a virus and no one can give it away. If there ever comes a time when you feel like you have to go someplace to find a better you and you're going any farther than the mirror, don't take another step. As long as you are looking toward anything but yourself, you'll always be headed in the wrong direction.

You have everything you need to master life, and you need *everything* you have. All your crankiness, cravings, arrogance, and attitude are necessary to put the skills you will sharpen to the test. So don't ever think that you have to figure out how to leave some parts of yourself behind or that you have to become a "certain way" first.

Taking Refuge

As black people with the history that we have shared in this country, we sometimes feel that our access and resources are limited for even the most basic things. And often, they are. So how could we possibly have what we need to be happy and peaceful in our lives?

Fortunately, the resources that we need to initiate change in our lives are plentiful and always available to us. We can see these resources as not just something we use, but as wonderful treasures that each of us can discover, explore, and make use of. It is only a matter of awareness, a matter of seeing them clearly.

Out of the many, many treasures that the world has to offer, there are three especially important ones. If we place the confidence of our hearts and minds in these treasures, they will provide us with a protective shelter, a refuge. Within that protective shelter we can be nurtured, and we can return there when we don't feel sure of ourselves or when our direction is not clear.

1. Teachers:
Those that have come before us

In Zen tradition, the idea of lineage and ancestors is very important. Lessons that have been learned are passed down from teacher to student. Students become teachers and again pass on the lessons that came before us. The long line of teachers is considered your lineage. These are your ancestors. We have a great deal of respect for ancestors, and offer thanks for their willingness to share what they have learned to help make our lives easier.

Teachers can come in many forms, but we can often begin at home to locate one. When they are whole and healthy, our mothers and fathers are there for us and serve as the first barrier of protection against some of the harsher aspects of life when we are not yet ready or able to handle them. Even though they may not be perfect, we still have a lot to gain from talking to our parents and hearing their perspectives on life. If alive, our grandparents are the same. They have lived more than twice as long as we have. We may feel that their views are old-fashioned or out of touch, but if we open our ears and make a practice of listening very deeply, we can hear how their experience 40, 50, or 60 years ago is exactly like our own today. Our elders have been through so much of it already; they can make your life easier if you open yourself up to listening. You may have been raised by your grandparents because your natural parents were not able to raise you or were just not there. Your grandparents, or your aunts, uncles, and next-door neighbors, or your teachers, then become like your parents. And we cannot forget our extended families and the ways in which they can help us to gain insight. They themselves are treasures that we should honor.

Our rich history of eloquent speakers, fiery activists, and prolific writers is a neverending source of inspiration for us. They have worked hard to seek truth. The work that they have already done provides insight that helps us to explore our own lives. Their work helps us to realize that we are not alone in our need to find a sense of ease and belonging. By sharing their personal experiences and their own sense of suffering and joy in many different forms, they give us greater access to resources that help us figure out what we are doing and the best way to go about it. The fact that our examples can be so different from one another is helpful, too, because we *are* very different. We need all the examples that we can get to be sure that we are somehow, in some way, on the right track and that someone before us has been in the same place that we are in now.

2. Teachings: That which we have been taught

The great thing about teachers is that what they teach reaches far beyond the teachers themselves. Teachings are the legacy of information and ideas that come from our teachers. Even better, teachings come in an infinite number of forms. There are traditional teachings in the form of written books, formal lectures, and instructional and how-to guides. There are lessons that appear in creative forms, like novels, poetry, painting, music, and storytelling. How many times have you read a line in a poem and realized that the writer had gone through the same things you have, and that you were no longer alone? Miles played notes that taught us that we have a deeper bottom than we may have known. Frieda Kahlo's paintings teach us something about self-reflection and the way we see ourselves.

There is so much that we can learn from the teachings that are available to us. It is important for us to take the time to find them and use them to our greatest advantage. In order to create space for ourselves in the world, we have to find the things that inspire us to grow. It is what inspires us that makes life worth living at all. If we have no inspiration, nothing that "breathes life into us," we get very small inside and cannot see the beauty in front of us. We don't engage the life we are in because it is not interesting to us. Our life doesn't feed us or even seem like we belong to it. Things that inspire us provide our reason for "living" rather than simply "existing."

When choosing what inspires us to engage our lives, we can't choose only the things that make us feel warm and complacent. We have to make an effort to find those things that compel us to locate a greater truth and that remind us that we are a part of the greater whole. If we don't try to do this, we can become passive, isolated, and distant. It is *so* empowering for people to be able to share and express their truth. It is equally important to be unswerving about seeking and refining what truth is to us.

3. Community:
Those for whom we are responsible

No individual can live alone, no nation can live alone and anyone who feels that he can live alone is sleeping through a revolution.
—**Dr. Martin Luther King, Jr.**

The last and most important treasure we have is our community. We need community to support us and be the proof that we are not alone.

One of the lessons that many of the greatest philosophers and thinkers came to understand is that the freedom and happiness of each of us has no meaning if we are not all free. Every single one of us has a responsibility to feed and nourish the rest of the community, in whatever way that nourishment takes shape. We serve our community in exchange for all the benefits it provides, and the sense of place and belonging that it gives us.

As people of color, we need to honor and sustain our community so that we can feel like whole individuals. Our own ability to fully express ourselves in the world is dependent on the strength of our connections to others. When we take care of our homes and our communities, we are taking care of ourselves. I'm convinced that a large part of our purpose in life is to be of service to the rest of us. This doesn't necessarily mean that you should volunteer at a soup kitchen or a crisis center. Those are worthy things to do, and good places to start being of service. But the ways to be of service are limitless. You can be of service as an artist that makes beautiful or thought-provoking paintings and drawings. You may be of service as a strong leader that has the presence that inspires people to action. You may provide humor or beautiful music that urges people toward a greater humanity and respect for one another. It really doesn't matter what you do, and it doesn't have to be grand, as long as you pursue it with a sense of sharing and service and you are happy doing it. This is what enriches our lives and makes us feel complete; that we are a part of our life, rather than just watching from way in the back of the room, barely able to hear or make out what's going on.

Very often, we forget this and work harder toward dividing our community than toward building and maintaining it. But without community, the feeling of being separate from everyone else grows and we soon begin to feel that we are completely alone and have nothing in common with anyone else. Community means "being with" others. Though we are very distinct individuals, each with our own likes, dislikes, patterns, and ways of being in the world, we are also very much the same. We all have feelings. We all want to be content in our life and not feel agitated by it. We all experience hurt, pain, and fear. We all have the capacity to love, and we all seek happiness, pleasure, and laughter. But we easily forget our shared humanity. We become self-important and forget about everyone else around us.

Even worse, when we do form a community we sometimes get to feeling that maybe ours is more special than others. We start to see people as being too different if they aren't just like everyone else, if they don't "fit in." If someone is different, then we shut them out. Maybe they go and form their own group and that group decides that *it* is more special. We have divided ourselves and we are now in competition. We have multiplied the problem. Now, instead of being individuals that feel separate and alone, we become big groups of separateness and aloneness. Soon, we form more and more sub-groups within the group. Next thing you know, competition between sub-groups develops and there is more divisiveness. There are many sub-groups that we can be parts of, whether by choice or not. The group that is rich, the group that is poor, the group that is middle-class. Those Republicans and these Democrats. The capitalists and the socialists. We categorize people according to how much money they make, what school they went to if they went at all, and how far in school they went. We make titles more important than the people that they are given to. We are divided into groups that separate us and classify us like cans in a grocery store, all stacked in neat little rows, divided according to the labels we wear around our outsides.

Instead of celebrating our uniqueness as individuals, we use our differences as excuses to divide us up into smaller and smaller groups. The ways of dividing ourselves are almost as infinite as the number of people we are. We can get so far away from our original community that we no longer feel we are a part of it at all.

I love flowers. Whenever I get the opportunity to go to another part of the country or the world, I am always amazed that there are so many different flowers. They come in an infinite number of shapes, sizes, colors, and textures. Some have strong, rich smells and some are delicate and whispery. When I am at home or money is thin and I can't go far, I take up my flower-watching at local botanical gardens or at parks. I never get tired of looking at them because there are so many varieties.

Flowers seem like people to me because even though they can be so different and be scattered all over the planet in places with different conditions and climates, they are all flowers. Everyone sees them that way. They bring pleasure to us when we see them simply because they are flowers. We may find that the striking beauty of orchids or the sweet, clinging smell of white Casablanca lilies is especially moving for us, but we don't decide that the others are not worth looking at anymore because of that. Though there are many different varieties, we see them first and foremost as flowers and appreciate them for being what they are.

The most exciting thing about our life, like the flowers, is how much diversity there is in everything. We should be grateful for the breadth of humanity and appreciate how precious and intrinsically valuable each of us is. It is our unique qualities that make us completely irreplaceable. As black folks we need to bring special awareness to the damaging legacy of separation and false distinctions. The divisions are products of a long history of experiences. The ways we have been treated and seen others treated because of their heritage or looks are deeply ingrained in us. Unfortunately, we have learned a habit of passing that negative history on. We seem prone to dividing ourselves into increasingly smaller sub-groups. It is the creation of these divisions amongst ourselves that causes us the most pain within our own community. It's as if it isn't bad enough already that we are a fraction of a greater population that has, at times, been hostile toward us. We proceed to further divide ourselves into groups according to what part of the world our ancestors came from. You're considered "different" depending on whether you are of Latin, Caribbean, or African descent. Those groups divide themselves further—the Caribbean-descended black folks are Jamaican, Bajan, Guyanese, Haitian, or Bahamian. The Latinos and African descendants do the same.

Physical traits have always been the source of particularly painful divisions amongst ourselves. Directly related to the distinction made between the white and black races and the ideas we place on that, skin color is still a very harmful divide. Some of us are of a deep and rich chocolate brown that is viewed by others as "too dark." Others of us come in warm, reddish hues and bright fairer tones that some call "redbone" and "high yellow." Contrary to the belief that there is some way that one "looks black," we fill the spectrum of color from the palest pale to the darkest dark and don't miss a beat in between. From the time that white slave owners divided us into groups in which fairer-skinned "house niggers" prevailed over their darker-skinned "field nigger" brothers and sisters, we have allowed skin color to be the Great Black Divide.

It does not stop with skin color. The list continues. We have wide flat noses or narrow, more pointed ones that make us look either "too African/black" or "too white." Thick, woolly, kinky hair is either being "natural" or having "bad hair," depending on who you ask. Curly or wavy hair can get you the "good hair" seal of approval or make you a half-breed, not to be trusted because you're not "really black." All the while, you spend your time thinking that the person on the other side of the fence has it easier when really, we're all tearing each other down in one way or another. It could make anyone trying to fit into the perfect box pass out exhausted from all the circles they have to run in.

We make decisions about where we want to live, what colors we want to wear, how we want to live our lives, who we want to love, and the shapes of our families. Some things that make us "the same" or "different" are very much about our personal choices, and those things are within our control. Other things are deeper and less tangible, and we don't really understand where they come from.

Even when I was very young, I just didn't like chocolate ice cream very much. I didn't know why I liked vanilla and didn't want to be forced to figure it out. All the kids seemed to like chocolate; it was everyone's favorite and I knew that eating my vanilla made me different. Still, if I was going to enjoy my ice cream at all, I knew that I just had to be different and eat my vanilla. Fortunately, everyone seemed to be comfortable enough with eating their own ice cream that the flavor I chose didn't matter to them. Of course it is likely that no one has been beaten up or ridiculed as a four-year-old for preferring vanilla to chocolate. It would be a crime to inflict physical or emotional pain on a child for having a preference that comes from some unknown place. But we have done that and worse to our brothers and sisters that have lived different lifestyles and loved different people than those that we would choose for ourselves. Instead of learning from the pain we suffer because of discrimination and adding to our collective strength, some of us get stuck in fear and refuse to move on. We allow the cycle of suffering to continue by inflicting pain on others. Once we are aware of this, it is an act of cowardice and it weakens the fabric of our community.

We have the power to choose not to let our beautiful diversity be a source of division amongst us. We have to see ourselves as having enormous strength because of the wealth of our resources. That wealth lies in our differences. We have so much to learn from each other based on our range of experiences. We can share our different perspectives as individuals to make the vision of the greater community wider and more inclusive. This naturally multiplies our possibilities.

We cannot afford to bog ourselves down in trying to force our community members to have the same ideas that we have. We cannot, will never, and shouldn't all share religious/spiritual ideas, political agendas, aesthetics, or any other traits that make us unique. We have to come together and recognize our shared human-ness. In this aspect, we are in the same position that everyone else is in. As black people, we are part of and connected to the larger, more diverse community of people of color. And as such, we are part of the greater world community. We are all interconnected and dependent upon each other. If we do not see this, we will continue to allow difference to be a dangerous divide for us and we will never achieve harmony amongst ourselves, much less as part of the greater whole.

For Buddhists, putting our trust in the three treasures—teachers, teachings, community—is called "taking refuge." I didn't like that term at first, because I considered myself a strong person and "taking refuge" sounded too much like hiding. I didn't want to hide.

I was also afraid. My differences, my separateness, my standing alone were the ways I defined myself. Entrusting myself to others, learning from the community I had left behind—those were challenges I hadn't planned on.

Going Home

The most difficult part of engaging in a Buddhist practice for me had always been the idea of doing it within a community. On the outside, I was friendly and communicated well with people. But that was something I had taught myself a long time ago to cover up the sadness and loneliness I had experienced earlier in my life. As I got older, I didn't feel that sadness all the time, but I realized that I still had a tendency to be by myself and do things alone. I spent my first two years as a Zen student meditating alone. Aside from occasional visits to the Zen centers, I learned what I could from books and magazines, and signed up for various newsletters that I devoured the minute they arrived. At home I set up a small room just for practicing meditation. I was very satisfied with my ability to find more and more "clear spaces" in my mind, but I had no way of knowing how to go deeper. So, after a while, I went searching for a Zen teacher who could help me. I had read that in Zen practice the relationship between a student and teacher is very intimate, so I took my search very seriously.

I found Sensei Pat Enkyo O'Hara, who leads a meditation group in Greenwich Village in New York City. I guess because of that and because Pat is so open and welcomes everyone, our *sangha*, or community, (which I've been with now for four years) seems like a misfit group. Village Zendo has a few lawyers and writers, a potter, a pathologist, some activists, a martial arts master, a few therapists, an architect, a finance wiz and some college students. Some of them have money and others don't. The ages range from 20 to almost 70. They don't seem to have anything in common at all. And when I first got there, everyone was white except for one very fiery Japanese woman whose spirit I really loved. I think I got used to this strange group because they were so different from each other, so I didn't stand out quite as much.

About a year later, I came to a very, very hard place in my life. I didn't know which way was up. The business that I had put all my heart into had failed. I moved out of the city to an isolated area in upstate New York. The roommate that I moved upstate with had once been a close and trusted friend, but when she moved out she took some of my things with her and left some of her bills behind. And finally, my relationship fell apart.

At first, I was so depressed that I stopped eating for nearly three weeks. I felt weak, dull, and disconnected from everything, as if I were not really alive anymore. It was as if I had stopped breathing and it would just be a matter of time before I collapsed. I had no money and was too depressed to find a job. My life was like a bad dream, and I was stuck in it. Having become accustomed to keeping my deepest feelings to myself, I was positive that no one could understand where I was and I was certain they didn't care. So I just stayed home, alone and miserable.

Then one day I received a calendar from the Village Zendo in the mail. In just a few days, the week long summer *sesshin*, or retreat, would begin. Sesshins are periods set aside for intensive meditation practice. You leave your daily life behind to take an opportunity to look deeply inside yourself and "touch mind." By that time, I was desperate to get out of the hole I was in. So, as strange as it seemed even to me, I went to stay in a big house with 30 or so people to try to be by myself, but not alone. I didn't think the retreat would solve my problems, but at least I would have to get out of bed in the mornings and there would be three meals a day. Thankfully, the retreat would be silent, so I wouldn't have to talk to anyone.

When I got to the retreat, I kept to myself and didn't look at anyone. I could barely see anyway. My eyes stayed heavy with tears that wouldn't fall. I was determined not to draw attention to myself, and I didn't want anyone to try to "fix it" for me. What was broken inside me was mine alone to deal with. Before I knew it, four days had passed.

When you are very, very sad, wounded in a deep place, it is not only impossible but futile to keep your suffering hidden. If trapped, pain eats away at your insides and destroys your spirit from there. So while I didn't run around looking for a shoulder to cry on, I didn't stuff my sadness or bite down on it to keep it in check, either. I was grateful that no one said a word to me. Even though my deep sadness was apparent, they did not try to comfort me. Once, during a break, I stood looking across the big lawn. I was completely engulfed by my sadness. Julia, a warm English woman who always managed to be taking care of our group, handed me a tissue. I hadn't even realized I was crying. She handed me the tissue without a shred of judgment and just as quickly left me to my own space.

That same day, I finally went to the private interview to talk with my teacher face-to-face. As soon as I sat down, I blurted out how screwed up I felt my life was, how I had failed miserably in so many ways and couldn't stand my own self anymore. I beat myself up for a few more minutes before she looked at me and said, "You have to be gentle with Angel."

Pat Enkyo O'Hara Sensei is a middle-aged Irish-American woman. *Sensei* is what Zen teachers are called. At the time, she was a professor of new media at New York University. In some ways, we couldn't have come from more different places. But she looked at me so knowingly, it was instantly clear that all the categories, labels, and differences were unimportant. She wasn't just looking at this young black woman sitting there with her face contorted with pain. We were not black and white or even teacher and student. We were just two human beings acknowledging suffering. Pat was seeing me *and* my pain. She was sharing my pain with me. In that moment and for the first time in weeks, I felt my despair lighten. I left the room noticing that I was finally breathing again.

That retreat was the beginning of not just healing the pain I was dealing with in that moment, but of opening my heart wider, expanding my vision farther than I had ever realized was possible. I had taken refuge in my teacher and my sangha. Through the simple acts of giving me just what I needed without asking for anything in return, Julia had pointed out to me that my dignity was still there. Pat, of course, taught me without teaching that I had to have compassion for myself in order to have compassion for others. Gentleness toward ourselves and others is too hard to come by. As for the rest of the people to whom I never said a word and who never spoke to me, by being silently supportive and allowing me the space I needed to both acknowledge my sadness and not be isolated, they collectively taught me that healing begins at home, and that home is wherever you make it. For the first time, I understood Community. Our strange group had become a family and a home for me without my ever noticing it. While I was the only black person in the group, I directly understood that it was not about people looking the same, doing the same things with their lives, or being the same at all. It was an agreement to be mutually respectful and supportive no matter who you were. Everyone agreed to serve the community in this way. And we all benefited.

Taking refuge was not hiding after all. It wasn't weak or even passive. It was placing my trust in my teacher, in the lessons I gain from my own experience, and in my community. When I needed them most, they all became a place in which I could begin to heal. When you are aware of what you are doing, placing your trust in someone or something takes a lot of courage. It's an act of bravery. It acknowledges that you are not alone in the world and that there is a connection between you and all things. It's like money in the bank. When we honor our community, maintain it, treat it like the precious treasure that it is, it returns our investment a thousandfold. Where can you get better results than that?

3

Three Serious Poisons

Changing our lives is like cooking a big, hearty soup, a big pot of broth into which we slowly add ingredients. We taste our soup every now and then to see what it needs—a little of this, more of that. We add ingredients and taste again, refining our soup until it has complete nutritional value so that we can become stronger.

The problem is that each of us has not only the good fortified ingredients in our cabinets, but also some poisons mixed in there amongst everything else that makes up who we are. Some of the poisons are less potent than others, but there are Three Serious Poisons, and the more of these we add to our great pot of soup, the less likely we are to have the nourishment and strength we need for our journey in life. These poisons are the obstacles. Much as we'd like to, we can't hide them in the corner.

The Three Serious Poisons are Greed, Anger, and Ignorance. Many of us try to define these words as narrowly as possible so that we don't get caught in their accusing glare. "I am not greedy," we may say to ourselves. Or, "I might get angry, but I'm definitely not greedy," and so on.

Greed

In truth, greed is the close cousin of lust. Lust is greed for another's body that is not fueled by genuine love, appreciation, or affection. Instead, the lust is fueled by the same force that causes people to hoard resources for themselves, for their own benefit or financial gain. In this way, they choke off the natural, even distribution of the world's resources. We often use the phrase "a lust for wealth and power."

Our greed and lust are not always so grand or large-scale as those of money-hungry, faceless corporations, but they are just as poisonous when they fuel a compulsive sense of wanting more and more of what we already truly have enough of.

Greed is present at all those times when we could have made room for other people in our hearts but instead remained stubborn or indifferent, withholding of our love as if it could get used up if we were free with it.

Greed is close by in all the moments when we could have made room for others in our minds but instead we refused to see their human condition as equally important to our own.

We are being greedy when we are driving and someone coming from a parking space or making a lane change wants to cut in front of us and we speed up right away to keep them from getting in. We are hoarding what we imagine to be our personal space. It is greed when we "collect" sex partners with a reckless disregard for the feelings and emotions of all involved. We say, "I can't make up my mind" or "I'm just a player" or the familiar "He (or she) is not giving me what I need, so I have to get it from someone else." We are treating our partners, lovers, husbands, and wives as objects. Rather than clearly seeing and treating them as whole human beings that deserve attention, affection and, most important, our presence, they become more like base-

47

ball cards, sneakers, or CDs that we collect, sort, maintain, and discard at our will. The problem here is that unlike things, people come with sets of feelings, and they have a right to be honored. We each have a responsibility to honor them.

I'm not advocating a particular type of relationship here, but more important, I'm in favor of intense honesty and respect in all areas of our lives—especially in our sex and love lives. If you are seeing one person here and another person there and cannot be honest with both people, then you would be better off sticking to just one. If you do make yourself available, if you are present with just one person and give him or her the attention you would have otherwise spread out amongst two or three people, there could be a reward. Sensing your presence and full attention, that one person may feel safe enough to be less greedy with their heart and you may find that you both have more of "what you need" to share with each other after all.

Anger

Anger is the poison that most of us can readily admit to having a close and often recurring relationship with. You may say to yourself, "Yes, if there's going to be a poison that ruins my soup, anger would be it."

Anger is the most obvious of the poisons; its potential dangers are easily seen. But for black people in this country, it is also easily the most complex. Many of us embrace what we consider our anger as the force that motivates the actions, and thus the changes, that benefit us as a people.

Isn't it our anger at and frustration with continued injustice that compel us to take to the streets to protest? Hasn't anger fueled some of the most important moments and movements in the history of the Diaspora? Our collective anger brought together and ignited a movement when Rosa Parks was made to leave a bus after refusing to give up her seat to a white woman. This poisoning anger has been our friend and protector, hasn't it? At least on the surface, that would appear to be true.

The harmful, poison anger that I am speaking of here is the kind that is the seed of hatred. Hatred as a tool has never accomplished any good. It is not so much a powerful feeling as a blinding one. Hatred cuts off our ability to see the humanity of others. When this happens, we no longer have regard for the basic rights of others. We do not honor their right to seek happiness, to pursue their dreams, to live decent lives.

Blacks in America have been especially wounded, damaged, and fragmented by hatred. This damage has come from blows inflicted on us by others, inflicted amongst ourselves, and aimed outwardly against other peoples. Nearly every single one of us has met with unfair treatment, subtle or severe, as a result of direct or indirect hatred of who we are as black people.

It is for this very reason that I am always deeply saddened by how many of us are able to use the same weapon of hatred against other so-called marginalized people, even while knowing the pain it brings. Gays, lesbians, and transgendered people suffer deeply as a result of this ignorance and fear-based hatred. Sometimes we single out other groups and make them the butts of our jokes. Every last one of these people is a part of our collective community. They are not "like" you and me. They *are* you and me. People who are racist are often so because of their lack of experience. Some were never taught better. And there are those who do know better and whose unfairness is intentional. No one is justified in causing another harm, but even the most hateful people are still human beings. They may need to be separated from general society for the protection of others and the good of the community, but even they do not deserve hatred, pain, or death.

To knowingly inflict pain on other people and cause them harm or suffering naturally brings suffering back home to us. Of course, it is at home, where things are closest to us, where we can see the poison of anger every day.

Anger and Intimacy

There was a brief time in my life during which I thought I had everything I wanted. I had a partner whom I loved deeply. I felt truly connected to another human being for the first time in my life. It was not a blind infatuation, but a mature love that developed and grew from working very hard on the relationship. It wasn't easy, either. We'd had misunderstandings, conflict, and jealousy between us, like so many people forming relationships do. But miraculously, we also had a deep and passionate love.

In fact, it was because we'd managed to come through the earlier difficult period that I was so proud and protective of what we had. I felt that if we were able to withstand and resolve some of our early difficulties, we would be able to withstand almost anything.

I think we were both thinking of our relationship as having long-term potential. Sometimes out loud, but mostly secretly, I admitted that this was a person with whom I could see myself for the rest of my life. I say secretly because it is often hard for us to admit, even to ourselves, that we would like to surrender our hearts to someone. But there I was, ready to give up my longtime habit of keeping the very tender core of me to myself. When you have felt betrayed, as many of us have, by people we thought we should be able to trust—mothers, fathers, teachers, lovers—it is particularly difficult to believe that you can trust again without living to regret it. It is then even more difficult to share the deepest things with your loved one, for fear that they might either become distant or abuse your feelings once they know that you are vulnerable. But once I made up my mind to work hard at being open, it was a great relief to begin to share my hopes with my partner.

I was happy in the other areas of my life as well. I felt that my spiritual practice was maturing. For work, I had begun a project that was meaningful to me and that felt in sync with what I wanted to do with my life. My partner and I were part of a close-knit group of five friends that had become like a family, something I felt I had missed in my life. We spent time together in different configurations, going to brunch, the movies, night-clubs, having drinks, or just watching videos.

I had matured enough by that time to no longer create illusions of perfection in my mind. At the same time, my life seemed laid out before me. It felt manageable, clear, and—for the first time in a long time—without crisis. My partner and I had developed the patience to work on our problems together and a common language in which to do it. I felt nourished by my relationship, supported by our friends, and whole in that I was at least working on all of the things that were important to me: my love, my work, and my practice. I was, in a word, content.

Then the proverbial walls came tumbling down. In what seemed like a day that would never end, my life, my love and my community did such a sudden flip that I could no longer recognize them as what I'd had a moment ago, could no longer see them as my own.

After a few days of sensing that something was not right, it became clear to me that my partner had betrayed my trust by sleeping with someone else. When I found out, I was numb at first, then incredulous, saddened, crushed. The walls of my world began to close in on me and I could neither breathe nor think straight. Part of me wanted to just run out the door and leave.

Somewhere inside, I knew that I should. But the part of me that was hurt and confused wanted desperately to stay—to find out what had happened and why.

My mind began to race with questions: How could this be? We were so connected, so in love. What had I done wrong? Why did I not see this coming? I wrapped my brain in endless circles looking for an answer to something that didn't make sense to me. I was very, very hurt, but I did not want to really acknowledge my pain. Instead, I became annoyed with myself for being caught out there. I wanted to make the pain disappear. So I did what so many of us are tempted to do when confronted with feelings that we do not want to face or situations we feel unable to handle: I had a drink. I found a bottle of vodka and some orange juice and made myself a drink. And then another and another.

I've never been a very good drinker, so by the time my partner came home, I was *well* on my way to being drunk. I had actually stopped drinking by then but the damage had been done. As the evening wore on, I became less and less aware of myself as the alcohol took its toll. In my frustration, pain, and eventually rage, I was no longer connected, no longer aware. My ability to see clearly was gone. I closed my eyes and allowed Anger to take over without even realizing it. Even if it was only for a few moments, it had been there. And I could not take back the damage that had been done.

Of course when I confronted my lover about the betrayal, the response did not satisfy me. But then again, how could it possibly? What answer would have made me happy? I didn't have time to think about that because before I knew it, the situation escalated and a bad situation became much, much worse.

To be honest, I don't really remember exactly how it happened. Was I provoked? Backed into a corner? Did I hit first? I've gone over the details in my mind ten thousand times in ten thousand ways. Some things I feel certain of, some things are not so clear. What I do know is that I was not there. Me, the person that I know, was not the person that was present that night.

In trying to avoid pain (which I had still felt piercing sharply through the haze of my drunkenness), I rendered myself unable to confront an important matter with a clear mind and, therefore, better judgment. I stayed overnight at a friend's house, and the next morning everything was still a blur. I could not believe even my own memory of what had happened. The next evening my partner and I met, talked, and looked each other in the eyes. Only then did I realize how severe it really was. We had gone to a place that seemed impossible for us to return from.

Fortunately, deep suffering can sometimes have the benefit of revealing to us what was there all along. What I came to understand as being more important than the details that contributed to the situation was the way in which I handled it.

When things are going well, it can be pretty easy to maintain balance and hold your head up high, proud of your good behavior. But it is during those times of suffering and confusion that we need to pay extra attention. It's when we have fallen down off our own pedestals and life doesn't come to us as easily that we most need to be present. I allowed my anger to rule my behavior. As a result, I lost my lover and by extension, our shared community of friends. The way I handled my anger caused me to lose the very things I loved most and wanted to keep. The scariest thing, though, was that I felt that by allowing my anger to control me, I had lost myself.

To be sure, there is a spirited power that comes from seeing what is wrong in the world and wanting to change it. The more we recognize how intimately connected we are, the more we ourselves suffer when we know other people are suffering. When we think about the unnecessary pain that people inflict on others, we may become angry, often because of our own unresolved pain. But it is not the feeling of anger itself that will make changes. It is how you respond to it. You can take the anger that you feel and make it productive rather than raging. You can use it as a catalyst for addressing wrong with great energy and power. But then, it is no longer anger, is it?

Ignorance

Ignorance comes in many forms. We think of ignorant people as people that don't know. Most racists are considered ignorant because they harbor their hatred based on false ideas that they have heard. Many white racists have never known a person of color. They certainly have not known them all. Their behavior and actions come from a place of ignorance.

Then there is intentional ignorance. Anything that we do to make ourselves unable to view circumstances clearly is intentional ignorance. For instance, my drinking at a crucial moment was intentional ignorance. I clouded my own vision. I could try to reason that the fact that I was drunk was why I could behave the way that I did. And it would be true. But it would not be taking responsibility for the fact that it was me that made me drunk. I went looking for the drink, made one, and sat and drank one after another. I knew well that I can't drink more than two drinks without becoming fuzzy. I can't make excuses for being unclear and not remembering how I got myself into the state I was in.

Finally, just the fact that we are unable to see things as they truly are is ignorance. We filter reality through our experiences, needs, and desires. We are fixated on the idea that because *we* see things a certain way, they must be so. We forget how many factors contribute to the way we see. Every single moment of our experience throughout our whole lives shapes the way we see the world.

We have cultural biases. In this country we eat beef on a regular basis and cows are considered stupid animals. In India, they are considered sacred and are never eaten. Some of us like our music loud and intense with a strong bass line. Others think of that as barbaric and prefer flutes or strings. We have differences based on how we were raised, whether we are Northern or Southern, if we come from the East Coast or the West. It is not that some of us are right and others wrong. It is just different perspectives, different experiences. Our eyes and ears, our senses of smell, taste, and touch and, most important, our minds play roles in how we experience everything we encounter.

The problem is not that we all have these different views of things, it is that we each consider our views the *only* reality. We forget that life is truly a matter of perspective. We delude ourselves by believing that our experience is absolute, fixed. The truth is that everything, including us, is changing all the time. Nothing is static, nothing is permanent. To believe otherwise because you see it as that way is to delude yourself. Delusion is ignorance.

We can see how greed, anger, and ignorance combined cover the entire range of that which keeps us from touching reality. They alone stand between us and our chance at enlightened being in the world.

Greed is clearly a product of desire. It is desire blinded and running rampant. And worse, it seems to be contagious. When we are greedy, that feeling spreads and contaminates everything. Our possessions become so important to us that they begin to take priority over people. It makes us feel as though we must protect what we have from others. We can become cold and hard. Because we have put so much energy into acquiring it, our "stuff" takes on imagined significance. We spend a lot of time looking over our shoulders making certain no one is coming to take away what we have, and we spend time looking over the shoulders of other people to see what they have, just to be sure they don't have something we want, or more of it than we have.

With greed in our hearts, we are unable to share ourselves completely with others. We cannot have generous spirits. We are afraid to give freely, worried that we will have nothing left. We are suspicious that almost everyone is out to take something away from us. Even if that something is love! In our desperation to get what we want, we may disregard and abuse the feelings of others. We become shortsighted, and all that is important to us is that we maintain our small space. We are terrified that we may have to share. With greedy hearts and minds, we shut our eyes in the interest of maintaining our own possessions. We shut our eyes to our world. Desire infests us, and the outcome is that we begin to lose our own humanity.

When we harbor hatred for others we rob them of their own unique identities and experiences of the world. Our own fears and insecurities make us hate ideas and people that are different.

Anger presents itself in many forms. It is almost always beyond our control, though. It is like a bully that comes in and takes over the situation and leaves no room for anything or anyone else. In our anger, we forget the other person's story. When enraged, we cannot feel our responsibility to the greater community because we are too busy giving attention to our anger.

When we are ignorant, whether passively or intentionally, we have no chance to see the truth for what it is. If it is a passive kind of ignorance, we move about in a foggy bliss of unawareness. This may seem inviting at first, but we continue to be subject to many discomforts and crises, although we don't know why.

If we make ourselves ignorant, if we actively delude ourselves, then we are making a terrible mistake. We rob ourselves of the clarity of truths. We miss the beauty as well as the full depth and worth of the universe.

Greed, anger, and ignorance have lived with us for a long time. They are like our friends or lovers. We wake them up, take them to work, and then take them to bed again. Even the idea of releasing them may be frightening to us. Secretly we say to ourselves: *My greed makes me pursue what I want aggressively and I am successful because of it. I like my anger, it makes me feel powerful. I like to get drunk because I lose my inhibitions, communicate better, and feel more attractive.*

Yes, these habits have been with us a long time. And though we may fear losing them, in our hearts we know that they are harmful to us. It is like bad relationships. We finally come to the revelation that they are no good for us. We are attached to them, so we may not want them to leave us. The habits are clearly unhealthy, and we know in every fiber in our being that we should move on, but we can only do that by letting them go. Only then can we begin to heal the damage that they have done. Only by letting them go can we become whole in a way that we have always known was possible, but have never had the chance to experience.

Part 11

steps
for creating
a spiritual
life

4

Awakening the
Warrior-Spirit

Let me respectfully remind you,
Life and Death are of extreme importance.
Time passes swiftly by, and opportunity is lost.
Each of you should strive to awaken, awaken.
Take heed . . . do not squander your lives.

—Evening Verse for Zen Centers

Ultimately, the reason each of us initially decides to "be more spiritual" or take up a spiritual path of some kind is because we want to get something out of it. That's a difficult thing to admit to and say out loud because it sounds like we are being greedy, wanting something for ourselves. We may want the benefit of escaping our pain and confusion. We might feel as if we will do better in life. Sometimes we hope we will be more prosperous and not encounter as many difficulties if we are more spiritual. Or we may just want to feel better about the person we look at in the mirror each day.

Whatever the underlying reasons, we start off on spiritual

paths with our minds already set on what the benefits may be. So, the more we hear about the need to be selfless and to stop filling our minds up with ideas about what we can get out of it, the more we feel conflicted because in the back of our minds we know that we *do* want something out of this. The problem is that you may not want to admit this even to yourself for fear of seeming selfish. Even though it doesn't sound all that noble, the real truth is that we don't want to just learn and practice and do spiritual work for no purpose at all.

Searching for Happiness

Human beings want to be happy. It's just as much a part of what makes us human as the urge to get up and walk on our hind legs. We have a need not just to live, but to thrive. At the most basic level, we need food and water for sustenance and shelter from the elements. We'd like to raise our children healthfully and in safe conditions. But as part of our human condition, we also have strong longings for community, intimate relationships, and fulfilling activity. And even though it may not seem like it when you watch television, we all really do want peace in our lives. We want to experience joy and love. We want a sense of purpose and belonging. To put it simply, we each want to feel satisfied with who we are and what we have. However we define it as individuals, we all want good lives.

My own sense of isolation is what made me investigate Zen Buddhism at first. Learning self-acceptance and gaining a sense of freedom have led me to make it a practice in my life. I want to be happy. I want my life to feel as if I belong in it and to it. That's why I choose to stay on this path. *Hey, wait a minute,* you're saying to yourself. *What about being responsible for everyone and being of service to the community? What about selfless giving to others?* Yes, now that I have gained a little more maturity, I know that I want to contribute to the world. I see the need to support my community. I feel that the purpose of my life is to be of service to the world I live in, and I take that purpose on with great joy and a sense of freedom. And I don't feel at all burdened by the idea of such enormous responsibility. I'm no longer attached to being a "this" or a "that," with a special name and those fine, flowing robes. I want to continue to deepen my practice so that my actions are thoughtful and come from a place of compassion. But that's definitely not where I began.

First and foremost, the thing that brought me to spiritual practice was a concern for me. That's not only okay, it's how it is for everyone, and it should be. It's our personal, individual concern that makes spiritual practice human. No matter who we are, where we come from, or what our cultural conditioning is, it's natural that practical results for our own lives are what we want from any spiritual practice we choose. We want to have better lives. If we can't face this truth we'll always harbor guilt. We will believe that our practice is flawed because it didn't come from the "right place."

The happiness that we want to experience doesn't mean that we need to have parties with balloons all the time or that we need to laugh and play 24 hours a day. It does mean that we want to feel that our needs are being met. Both inside and out. We want balance in our lives and want to feel content. This wanting comes from deep within us and is what motivates and inspires us to continue to live each day. It is the deep inner need to feel content that sets us out looking for spiritual direction. We have to celebrate that, both as human beings and as black people. We need to know and accept from the start that it is the simple human desire to be happy that makes a spiritual path not only fulfilling, but worth pursuing in the first place.

At a deeper level, if we hold on to an idea about what the right way to be spiritual is, we may never see ourselves as ready or worthy enough to step out onto a path. We could walk around with the idea that there are spiritual people and non-spiritual people. Until we perform a magical feat, have some mystical experience, or find ourselves in church every day, we may see ourselves as part of the non-spiritual group. Even if we have a conscientious practice, we may give our power away to self-doubt. We are concerned that we don't go to church, temple, or retreats enough. Leaders of spiritual groups and traditions sometimes encourage our doubt about our own ability to achieve greater spiritual understanding. We are led to believe that only by going to church, temple, or mosque can we find peace. We sometimes think that only our reverends, rabbis, and roshis hold the key.

But we can't let that happen. We can't allow ourselves to give that authority away to anyone. There's no separation between our spirits and our lives. We are the only ones who can wake ourselves up to seeing that. We need to realize that each of us holds the key to our own freedom. All along, right from the beginning, through the middle and up to this very moment, you are the gatekeeper to your own happiness. If you want to experience heaven on earth, you have to manifest it for yourself. And in the long run, there's really no point to any spiritual or secular path or training that doesn't show you that the way to freedom is to surrender your ideas and concepts and wake up to the life that you have right now. The most important and only truly valuable thing that any book or teacher or guide can do is to point to that fact over and over again. Teachers can offer us a framework or guidelines for seeing this truth for ourselves, but whatever our spiritual reference point may be, and no matter how gifted and wonderful our teachers are, they can only help us to see that the experience of personal freedom has to be direct and intimate so that it becomes our own. No one can give us the answer. It all begins and ends at home.

Life as a Warrior

The man who became the Buddha was known as Gautama, and he was born into a warrior clan known as the Shakyas. Historically, there has been an emphasis on the idea that the Buddha was a prince. He was, in that he had significant wealth, wore fine robes, and enjoyed overflowing feasts. But he wasn't what we would call a prince today. He wasn't in line to rule over an entire country like a Prince Charles ascending to the throne of England. Gautama's clan wasn't even the biggest clan in ancient India, but warriors were highly esteemed because they served a very special role. Rather than being a group that terrorized or caused havoc, warriors had the responsibility of protecting the people. A warrior was considered of the highest class next to saints and priests. Because of this, and owing to the peace they brought to their community, they were like royalty.

But even before Gautama was born as a Shakya warrior, he had been a warrior of another kind. In previous lives, Gautama had been a *bodhisattva*. Bodhisattva means "awakening being" and refers to a person of any culture that is brave and willing to walk on the path of wakefulness. Bodhisattvas don't have to be fully awake themselves. They are awakening warriors that give up floating through life aimlessly and being concerned only with themselves. Awakening warriors live in a way that is of benefit to all, and their work is done here in this world. They see that we must all take responsibility for ending suffering, not just for our own individual freedom, but for that of others as well. What these awakening warriors realize is that in order to live harmoniously and with joy, they must take their natural place in the world.

Does this mean that in order to live with more joy and grace and less fear and anger we need to run out and take up arms or develop aggressiveness and a warlike stance? Not at all. What we want to do is embody the spirit of a warrior and bring that to function in our daily lives. "Spirit" refers to that which gives life. "Warriors" live a life of action and clear direction. We can bring warrior-spirit to the cause of peace and harmonious connection because it is about life and living, not power and aggression. Warrior-spirit is also free of religious form. It's free of dogma or a set of rules that we have to follow. We can manifest warrior-spirit within our faith in Christianity, Sufism, Buddhism, Islam, Yoruba, or any other religion. It is a way of being, but not a *new* way. There are guidelines that we can use, but all the directions point to a place that is already within us. Warrior-spirit is a frame of mind that lets us make a habit of cultivating the qualities and skills that are already available to all of us.

To put this into a context: We have the choice to remain in ignorance and convince ourselves that we are safe from the sight of others' pain, or we can choose to develop our warrior-spirit. We can acknowledge that the road may not be easy, and then we can put our best foot forward anyway. When our uncertainties and fears are getting in our way, we can acknowledge them and say to ourselves:

- I want to be awake.
- This is my intention and I am fully aware that it will require me to make an effort that I may not be accustomed to.
- However, I no longer want to feel stuck in my own life.
- I want to be able to feel connected to my community.
- I am ready to be open and fully engage everything that comes my way. I want to touch reality, become intimate with it, and see my life with vivid clarity.
- I know that it will not be easy and I will have to face aspects of myself that I may not be proud of.
- And, even if I feel afraid of this, I am confident that I am worthy of living life in the fullest way possible.
- I am sure that I deserve to know an enlightened way of being in the world.

That's warrior-spirit. When all is said and done, what is most important is the action that you take. You can say a thousand prayers, do ten thousand prostrations, or wish a million times for freedom, peace and a stronger, wiser you, and that would be very empowering. But it's the day that you lift a finger to help, open your ears to hear, and raise your voice to advocate truth that you have taken a step toward freedom. In life, there is only activity or passivity. Being active in our lives is a conscious choice that we must make and then follow up on to the best of our ability.

The Bodhisattva Vows

Gandhi said that "vows prepare us for adversity." Like affirmations, they give us a reference point for strength when we feel tapped out. We also make vows to help remove the limitations that we usually place on ourselves. We want to be able to be generous and open with our families and loved ones. We also want to develop our sense of responsibility for everyone we share the earth with, and such sharing is what will most contribute to a global harmony that enriches all our lives.

Every evening, all over the world and in numerous languages, Zen Buddhists chant what is known as the Bodhisattva Vows. The traditional Bodhisattva Vows are a powerful expression of the spirit of what it means to be an awakening warrior. Each one is a promise to do something that, at first, sounds impossible. That isn't to make us feel defeated. It works to encourage an energetic charge into daily action in our lives. The vows are chanted three times as a reminder that we must actively work to reduce suffering in our lives. Voices are raised in a harmonious commitment to collective responsibility for the freedom of everyone that is in pain. The Bodhisattva Vows can be chanted as part of a group ceremony, or they can be just as useful at home.

Steps for Creating a Spiritual Life

. . .

BEINGS ARE NUMBERLESS, I MAKE A PROMISE TO SAVE THEM.

There are a lot of people and animals and insects living on this big floating ball together.

We may think of the planet as fixed in size, but we know that everything is relative. Even if the planet is not shrinking, the fact that there are more and more of us on it has the same effect as if it were growing smaller. You know that when you live with people, it is very important to get along. If not, no one ever rests well. It's the same when you live in a house with someone that you have conflict with or dislike. You may have separate rooms, but you never really relax because you're busy thinking about how much you don't like the person. Just carrying those negative feelings can wear you out. Maybe you're even thinking some harsh thoughts about them, wishing they didn't have the right to live there too. But they do and so you feel like you just have to live with that. How awful! That's what that word "tolerance" feels like to me. You just kind of put up with someone because they are there and you don't have much of a choice.

Well, it's true, we are all here. But it's not true that we have to tolerate people because they are here. They are not *just here*. Nobody is "just." We are here sharing space. We are sharing resources, the air that we breathe. So rather than "just here," we are co-existing, co-living, co-being here. And as the planet gets smaller, it becomes more and more clear that none of us are free-floating and inconsequential. That may be the way we feel sometimes, but it really isn't so.

One of the major dilemmas that so many of us face is a sense of separation from the rest of the world. We have either lost or never really had a sense of intimacy with one another. I don't mean sexual intimacy, or even the intimacy that comes from actually getting to know people and becoming familiar with them. It is intimacy with the entire world that we are missing. This is what makes us feel distant and separate. When that happens, we stop noticing what is in our environment and everything becomes part of the background. In this way, we miss the details of our lives. We do not see the brilliance of the setting sun or the glory of the full moon. We forget our childlike fascination with the colors of a butterfly. Everything seems just like everything else because we've stopped really looking.

Somehow we believe, even if subconsciously, that random, meaningless people are everywhere, living their random, meaningless lives. We do not have the energy to pay them any attention until they enter our lives. That is when they become noticeable to us. When they affect us they become important only because we think we are important. It makes perfect sense that when someone or something disturbs our decidedly important lives, we can become angry. We are angry because we have a set way of seeing life and have decided how it should function. When it does not meet our expectations, we feel that our plan has been upset. It works like this in our subconscious minds: "I have certain perceptions about life, and how dare you not operate by them and present your own way instead? You are not behaving according to my set of concepts. Because I cannot accept that there are different ways of being other than what I expect, I am now angry with you." Our anger then makes us feel hostile. We see the person or thing that has upset us as separate from us. She, over there, rolled her eyes at Me, over here. We think of ourselves as completely separate beings so it is okay for us to be angry or hostile. We are not aware of how incredibly connected we all are.

What makes us angry is that we cannot see the infinite number of ways there are for the world to present itself. We believe only in our own reality. We see our own individual selves as the center of the universe. Many, many times, the anger is not even directed at an "other." It is really intended for ourselves. We become angry with ourselves when we do not know what to do with our fears. We impose the same set of expectations about the way things should be on ourselves. When we are not able to meet our own expectations, we can become especially angry. It is very, very difficult to face ourselves when we find we cannot meet our own expectations.

We respond to our disappointment in different ways, depending on our personal experience, how we are raised, and the models we have for handling things. Some of us are very obviously angry with ourselves. We complain and beat ourselves up. "There is just no excuse for not getting that promotion. There must be something wrong with me. I am a loser and I must not deserve to have it." We may punish ourselves in the same way that we try to punish people that we feel angry with.

On the other hand, we may not show our anger with ourselves outwardly at all. We may be the type that holds the self-anger inside because we are so afraid of what it means to be very angry with ourselves. Instead, we move around in the world stuck in our anger. We carry it on our faces. It reveals itself in the stiffness of our bodies. We may speak through clenched teeth. Our behavior toward other people may be terrible because the anger is stuffed down inside us and we don't want to see it, so instead it directs itself outwardly. But we can't wish it away. When anger is there, it is there. To ignore it is futile because it will reveal itself in some way. If it must show itself in a forceful, misdirected way in order to be seen, it will do that. That was apparent to me when I struck out at my partner. I was hurt and angry and unable to give those feelings the attention they needed, so instead, they presented themselves in an uncontrolled, misdirected way.

It is possible that we don't realize that the anger is really meant for ourselves. This can create the most fiery, unpredictable, harmful anger there is. Because you are afraid to meet face-to-face with the anger inside you, you avoid it. You avoid dealing with your own inner self. You see the anger as separate from you in the same way that you see people as separate from you. Instead of "me, here" and "them, there," you feel "me, here" and "that anger, there." The anger is not you, but it is not separate from you. If you try to remain separate from the anger, you will only create separation from yourself. The *most* intense feeling of separation you can have is the feeling of separation from You.

The vow to save everyone acknowledges that you are not alone here. When you take this vow you agree to participate in the collective effort for a better life for everyone, for saving every one of the numberless beings. We save our children and lovers from our anger by being clear on where the anger comes from and not allowing it to control our actions. We do not let our anger define how we interact with other beings or even with ourselves. We do not allow the anger to create a false sense of separation. We start to practice being more aware. And it isn't even very hard.

Beings are numberless. With practice, I promise to notice them and see that there is no separation between us. In this way, I contribute to saving them all.

· · ·

DESIRES ARE UNCEASING, I MAKE A PROMISE TO END THEM.

It can give you a headache just thinking about how many times a day your mind goes chasing after some real or imagined desire. The serious: *I just want to go home and get in bed, I am so exhausted.* The longing: *I want some mashed potatoes with half a stick of but-*

ter, even though I know better. And the plain old picky: *Why do they keep it so cold in here? . . . My feet hurt . . . . Why does she chew her gum like that?* It's just like that, too. A ceaseless, neverending stream of desires all mixed up together and all competing for our attention at once.

But we do have needs, don't we? I, for one, can get over the gum-chewing, but what's wrong with some extra butter every once in a while? The big question is: If I just sit here not wanting anything, wouldn't I stop being a person? That's just not human. Maybe some religious fanatics are on that trip, but I can't go there with them. A desire can appear instantly: BANG! There it is! When we think of not having desires, we're afraid we will disappear. Why is that? To get straight to the point: Because our desires are so persistent and so constant, we think we *are* our desires. And that shows how really, really attached to them we are.

Everybody wants something. It's true. As humans we all have cravings. We all have desires. I was listening to a tape not long ago in which Sharon Salzberg, a popular Buddhist teacher, talks about how His Holiness the Dalai Lama, the spiritual leader of Tibet, was at a big function and told everyone that even though he had been offered cheese, he really wanted cake. After he said it, he burst out laughing at himself. That's warrior-spirit too because it acknowledges that as awakening warriors, we are human, not Buddhas or God or saints. We will not suddenly become perfect models of control and we don't need to.

None of us escapes desire, and we don't want to escape. That is not the point. We would just like to stop holding on to them for dear life. We want to see them for what they are. They are cravings. They are desires. They do not own us. They do not need to force us in every possible direction, contorting our bodies to chase down the next thing. I won't be a captive to my desires, helpless in their power. More important, I won't make myself miserable because of my attachment to my wants, so miserable that to not satisfy them wrecks me. I won't let my full awareness of this moment be dragged on a roller-coaster ride for the next hour or even 15 minutes. I won't cling to my wants, needs, and cravings.

The strength of our desires is undeniable. We can often feel powerless when it comes to reeling them in. We may feel that we have to have a battle with them if we want to get anywhere at all. But becoming aggressive with our desires or anything else that arises is not the best way. Our intention is not to just beat them down until they are in little pieces. Our intention is to develop the art of living with our cravings and putting them in balance with our real needs. First, we want to coax them out into the open so that we can get a really good look at them. Very much like people, desires need to be noticed. Under scrutiny, a lot of desires will just fizzle, whether it's things (like more clothes or new house décor) or people (like more attention from our friends, and children who mind us). When we actually pay attention to them, we begin to notice that so many of our cravings just don't hold water. They may be the product of past experiences that we haven't yet released. Getting ourselves wrapped up in them is just a habit.

Just Enough

The whole idea of Zen retreats is to create an environment in which you must pay attention to every moment. You have to be present and aware in order to know what you should be doing and when. One kind of bell wakes you up in the morning. Another lets you know when it is time to start your meditation. Yet another rings when it is time to end. Activities are designed to help us focus and notice every detail. There is even a specific practice for eating.

Oryoki is the name given to formal meals, and literally means "just enough." Like everything at the entire retreat, eating is done in silence. There are servers that come around and offer each dish to everyone. You can signal for the server to give you as much or as little of each of the three dishes as you'd like. But there are no seconds and you're expected to eat whatever amount you have put in your bowls. So you have to request "just enough." When I first read about this practice, it didn't seem like a big deal. I thought it was a beautiful idea that we make a habit of eating only what will make us feel satisfied and not leaving any to waste. The first time I got to participate in oryoki was at *zazenkai*, a one-day meditation intensive. I was intent on making sure I requested just enough.

Everyone is served and waits for everyone else so that we can all begin eating at the same time. The servers offered brown rice, a great-smelling mixture of garlic and greens, and an apple-raisin dessert with soft oats mixed in. As the server's first spoon of rice hit my bowl, I thought about the fact that I hadn't eaten much earlier so I should get just a little more so that I wouldn't be hungry and irritable later. Greens aren't really filling and I never seemed to eat enough when I'm alone, so I made sure to get a serving that would be satisfying and be in balance with the rice. Finally, I've always liked apples and raisins together and I figured this would be the last meal of the day. I signaled for an amount that looked fair and not overwhelming.

I was only halfway into the greens when I realized I was in trouble. I didn't know if it was the nervous energy from doing my first all-day retreat, but I knew what I had in my bowls to eat was too much. Not wanting to seem as if I had just been greedy, I stuffed it all down. When I looked up, everyone was finished with their meals. They had all been waiting for me.

It was only a little embarrassing and I didn't think much about it until the next time I did oryoki, this time at a week-long retreat. To my own amazement, every single day, for three meals a day, I would get too much. My bowls were never overflowing or even filled to the brim, so it was hard for me to understand why it kept happening. Before each meal I would say, "Okay, this time I'll get it right" and almost every time, it seemed like everyone ended up waiting for me.

Early in my life, my parents separated and I ended up with my father. The two of us lived together for several years and we were thick as thieves. When I was eight, he remarried. My stepmother had a daughter already and soon my brother was born. After a while, I no longer felt that I got the attention I needed. My father's attention was divided between his work, his new family members, and the demands of a newborn child. I had to make do with the painfully little individual attention I received.

What the practice of oryoki made me realize is that I still carried with me that childhood sense that I wouldn't get enough. In my subconscious, I was deeply concerned that I would not be satisfied by whatever was placed before me. Even though I was considered a generous person with others, my habit was to feel overanxious about making sure I wouldn't go unattended to. I had an inner sense of poverty that I tried to make up for in many different places in my life, even in my Zen bowls. When I finally took the time to pay attention to how I was *feeling* rather than making infinite calculations about what "just enough" should be, I didn't request too much, and I wasn't ever hungry, either.

It is so important that we pay attention to the feeling that is speaking to us and not rush to classify it according to habit. How many times do we say, "I need to get something to eat" when we really mean, "I'm feeling anxious and I don't like feeling this way so I will do something to occupy myself"? If we look closely at the desire that came up, we see that it is not hunger that we are feeling, it is anxiety about the difficult feelings we keep trapped inside. The anxiety and discomfort we feel masquerade as desires. What we end up with is a relatively small number of true desires. Those few, we may choose to indulge—as long as we don't have a fit if we find that we are not able to. We just let them keep moving along. We let them fall away.

Putting an end to cravings is as easy as noticing them. We practice seeing them for what they are, and what they are not. We let them fall away. Like early autumn leaves, our cravings start off strong and bright. They hold on firmly. With time, as the soft winds of our practice work on them, they first fade and then fall away. Little by little, and at first, almost unnoticeably. But at some point you look up and the tree is bare. It is a very authentic view of the tree, fully open and exposed. You are seeing the tree completely as itself because the leaves, that at one time seemed to be the tree itself, have fallen away.

Desires are ceaseless. With practice, I promise to become aware of them, notice them, and allow them to fall away. In this way, I let them pass and put an end to them.

. . .

THE TRUTHS ARE WITHOUT LIMIT, I MAKE A PROMISE TO MASTER THEM.

The truths that make up the nature of life are completely without limit. There is no end to the knowing that is possible. This is the promise you make to be as vigilant in your effort to acquire knowledge as is possible for you at any given moment.

Black people and other people of color really need to be active in their analysis of both their individual situations and the situation of their communities. We each need to become even more engaged than we are. We need to participate in the world and have our voices heard beyond our own backyards, streets, and neighborhoods.

We cannot afford to be lazy thinkers, because there is too

much to be lost when we take that route. If we are not careful to think about the situations that we see around us, we cannot address them. Part of enlightened being and living responsibly is acknowledging that we are essentially in a relationship with the rest of the world. If we leave ourselves in a position in which we can't respond to the needs of others, we contribute to a breakdown in communication, in harmony, and in peace. This is how we create dysfunctional relationships in our lives, the lives of our families, at our jobs, in our communities and in the world.

Constant, active, critical thinking is crucial to our well-being. Too often, we take the position that it's "none of my business," which is a very dangerous way of thinking. Everything is our business, ultimately, because we are inextricably intertwined with everyone. To say that the war or genocide that is taking place on the other side of the Atlantic Ocean is none of our business does not make us free of responsibility. It simply denies our place in the world. When we say "I'm not going to deal with that because it has nothing to do with me," we are saying, *I haven't taken responsibility for engaging my community. I don't belong here.* But of course we do belong.

If we encourage this lazy way of existing, we become as harmful as the people waging the war. Blacks in America, like other persecuted and oppressed peoples in history, have a unique vision. Our history of both subtle and profound suffering has no doubt sharpened our sensitivity to the suffering of other people. We have powerful voices when we raise them and insist that we be heard. Too often, though, we remain silent. But it is a selfish kind of silence. We believe we are protecting our own freedom by not raising our voices for others, when really, when we are silent, we are giving our freedom away. Our full participation in every aspect of life is not only important, it is essential.

Active thinking is the key concept here. Of course we are always thinking. But is too much of our thinking passive and boxed-in? We may think we have bought in to the "American Dream," and that isn't so bad. From the beginning, though, that Dream's foundation was built on the backs of our ancestors. The Dream was not for us then. Now, 140 years after being freed from legalized slavery and 30 years after obtaining equal rights on paper, in many areas of life we are still not offered the same welcome as others are. In many ways, it is clear that whether intentionally or ignorantly, we are not invited to share in the Dream. By its own definition, an American Dream that is not inclusive of every single American regardless of race, color, gender, sexual orientation, cultural background, or religious/spiritual affiliation, is not the dream it was intended to be. For many people of color in America, it is more like a myth that holds only an unkept promise.

This myth is sometimes recreated in an especially "black flavor" by the marketing machine of America. Having discovered how brand-conscious and loyal we are, special attention is paid to making sure we remain attached to the idea of the Dream.

Here is a truth that many people in America don't bother to ever think about: Our country is not the center of the world. We are temporary visitors on the planet just as everyone else is. We have no greater rights or lesser rights than anyone or anything here. We are not any more or less privileged than any other beings anywhere. That includes people of the so-called Third World countries and of the African Diaspora. This is not politics. This is just truth. We have let the wealth of our nation's corporations alter our perspective so that we do not see this. Can we see this for what it is? Can we really see it?

All people have truths that relate to where they are in their lives. The truth of one person's poverty is equally and simultaneously as true as the truth of someone's wealth. The wealthy person is not inherently bad or good. Neither is the poor person. That is each of their truth, for the moment. Conditions change. The truth of this moment may not be the truth of the next. There is constant movement. Still, we have to honor this moment, because we do not know what the next one holds. And the truth of the past is, well, in the past. The only way to be truly honest is to stay completely in the moment that we are already in. And then the next, and the next. Every single being's truth and the truth of every given situation are all happening at the same time, moment to moment to moment, radiating out into every direction, dynamically creating new truths as they go.

You can see how there is no limit to truths. We should be prepared to master all of them. In being prepared to accept any and all truths, we are able to relax and be in our lives as they are. If we are willing to accept truth just as it comes, without trying to change it to suit our needs, we become free of the anxiety that comes from the urge to change and control. By master I mean receive with our full minds, open and without resistance. It doesn't mean that you know everything. Rather, it means that you may not know anything at all in a situation, but you have become so open to the infinite possibilities that you can approach and accept anything. Even pain. We have to be just as willing to touch and acknowledge the pain as we are to feel the joy. Why? Because one doesn't exist without the other. Who needs "up" if there is no "down"? They are so linked together that they are the same thing; different perspectives on the very same thing.

Whether you see a staircase as heading up or down depends on where you are standing. It is your perception of the situation. The concepts you have based on your experience with staircases get mixed up in the way you see things, too. You classify the staircase the way you do because you see it only from your perspective. The fact that you see it as either up or down is because you haven't practiced becoming open enough to see from all perspectives. When you do see from all sides you will not see either one anymore. The staircase is still the staircase no matter what angle you are seeing it from. No up and no down. Just the staircase as it is.

It works the exact same way with life. We are always deciding what things are and applying labels to them and then believing those labels just because we put them there. We forget that they come from us. We forget that the fact that we applied them doesn't make the labels true. It's okay that we forget, especially when we haven't had the opportunity to see for ourselves that there is a different way of viewing the world. Again, we don't want to go try to hijack truth so that we can master it. This should never be an angry or forceful process. We just practice. I would even encourage you to be s-l-o-w about it. There is no hurry to get somewhere.

Without a promise to master the truth, you invite ignorance to remain in its place. It is because the truths of this world are relative and ever-changing that we make a promise to master them.

The truths that make up reality have no limit. With practice, I promise to be an active and engaged thinker, open to the entire spectrum of possibilities, giving myself tools to work with. In this way I will master them all.

. . .

THE PATH TO ENLIGHTENED BEING IS UNATTAINABLE, I MAKE A PROMISE TO ATTAIN IT.

Each of these promises or vows directly affects one of the poisons, or obstacles; they all relate taking action to become aware. If we commit ourselves to greater clarity, we can live our lives with a warrior-spirit of scrutiny, honesty, and openness.

When we notice our anger, it gets broken down and begins to dissolve. The sense of separation that we feel between ourselves and everyone else dissolves with it. With that distance gone, real intimacy with the world is possible. We need that intimacy in order to feel comfortable. Once we are intimate with our world and our life, we can relax more in it. We notice the world beyond our small space. We become aware of everyone else in it. That awareness makes us responsive to their pain. This means that we have begun to take responsibility for everyone else. We have begun to save them all.

When we notice our cravings and can distinguish between real and imagined needs, we begin to see that they are not all necessary. We don't have to respond and react to every one. Our desires begin to fall to the wayside and leave us more open to seeing what is going on in the world. We no longer spend our time chasing down every whim. We are able to be less suspicious about what others may want from us or take from us or prevent us from having. That leaves us more clear and no longer weighed down by the anxiety of whether or not we will get what we want. We feel lighter. Like the tree, we can show a truer face and be more honest, more real with ourselves and with everyone around us. We become more authentic. The more authentic we are, the less we are victims of our cravings. Soon enough, we will have ended them all.

Finally, when we notice the infinite number of truths that contribute to the reality we experience, and we do not attempt to limit them with our own perceptions, our minds and hearts open wide. With open hearts and minds, we are more able to be active thinkers because we are less fearful of what the outcome may be. We can trust ourselves to perceive truth. The more we trust ourselves, the less likely we are to cloud our experiences or remain ignorant. Willing to accept any truth that comes our way, we begin to master them all.

The last vow, the vow to exist as an enlightened being, is like a gift, because the first three vows have revealed the truth of attaining it. You are already closer to an enlightened way of being in the world. Your potential for being more open has now expanded. You probably already feel a little lighter just knowing that there is some kind of answer to feelings that may have plagued you at one time or another in your life.

Enlightened being is not something you can pick up and put in your purse or knapsack like this book. It is not tangible. You cannot hold it in your hand or pass it around. You cannot put it down. The path to it is just doing. Just being. Just starting. It is action. Action itself is energy and cannot be "seen." We may see the effects of action or see action performed, but we do not see action. It is not an object. You can't get it and you can't get rid of it. So the path, in this way, is unattainable. Not get-able. Yet it is do-able. It is be-able. It is certainly start-able, and we know this because we have already started. We begin practicing the moment that we open ourselves up enough to pursue any path toward greater clarity. It is an integral part of us already, mixed into the fibers of our being. We are never separate from the intention of enlightened being. We may try not to touch it because we are afraid of the unknown, but it is here. In this way, we have already begun to attain it.

The path that leads to enlightened being is unattainable. With practice, I promise to realize that I have already begun to move in a direction that will clarify the way in which I see things. I am already more likely to notice things that have gone unnoticed before. It has already made me more aware. The path is not under my feet but a part of the enlightened being that I already am. In this way, I will attain it.

Warriors of Awakening

When we make a commitment toward enlightened being, we are at once taking on the responsibility and already fulfilling it. To inspire our way we have in our history a fine legacy of people who voiced a commitment to live more responsible lives. They were awakening warriors in their own time and many of them sacrificed what we consider elements of their personal freedom in the course of remaining true to their commitments of waking up the world.

Sojourner Truth was one of the first voices of both women's rights and human rights. She did this at a time when it was definitely not fashionable and could be life-threatening. She spoke up for black women to black men and claimed our place alongside them rather than behind.

Muhammad Ali, in what seemed a paradox coming from someone who made his living fighting in an arena, committed himself to denouncing war. As both a black man and a Muslim, he refused to be made to fight in a war against other people of color that was not his own undertaking. He was put in jail and lost his right to box, and with it his right to earn a living at his chosen profession. But he was unwavering, and his commitment outlived the war. He returned to become one of the greatest boxers the world has ever known.

Pierre Toussaint was a Haitian-born black slave that came to this country and lived with his "owners" as a domestic slave. In what may seem illogical to some, he took personal responsibility for the care and well-being of the woman that once "owned" him who had become poor after her husband died. She freed him before her own death, and Toussaint went on to take care of orphaned children, both black and white. Saying, "He lived in an outstanding way, better than we do . . ." the Roman Catholic Church continues to pursue his candidacy as the United States's first black saint.

Mohandas K. "Mahatma" Gandhi's steadfast pacifism is well-known throughout the world, and his name is synonymous with peaceful resistance. Over a period of nearly three decades, he "actively resisted" his way peacefully and responsibly into gaining political freedom for an entire nation of people. Most significant is that the sheer number of Indian people and his immense popularity gave Gandhi the opportunity to use force if he so chose. But above and beyond his insistence that nations of people have the right to their own political self-determination, Gandhi was committed to attaining his goal peacefully and responsibly.

El-Hajj Malik El Shabazz, also known as Malcolm X, had an amazing journey through life before arriving in a place of responsible living. He had the opportunity to experience many different ways of being. A petty thief, a hand-chosen protégé of a formidable organization, a charismatic leader, a powerful and feared activist, and finally a spiritualist, he was a man who sought and found a fundamental truth: The color of our skin alone neither defines us nor needs to be the cause of our separation. We are connected to each other and thus it only makes sense for us to live peacefully with one another.

The list of people that have made a conscious choice to be more responsible in life goes on and on. Their warrior-spirits transcended all boundaries of race, class, gender, sexual orientation, culture, and religious affiliation. Some are living and some are dead. They are all human. None of these people has been perfect, and there is no need to believe that we need to be either. It is the fact that they are human, have flaws, and make mistakes that makes it so clear that we can all do this. They represent the range of what can happen when a decision is made and action follows. What they all have in common is that at some point in their lives they *started*. It may have been early in life, or it may have taken decades for them to begin. With a warrior-spirit, the action one takes is all that matters. It only matters that they began.

Each time we commit to seeking truth, we awaken our warrior-spirit. We challenge ourselves to step beyond our sense of just-self-preservation and acknowledge our collective humanity. Embodying the warrior-spirit invites thoughtful action to be a part of our daily expression. We let openness and unattached giving inform every act. Best of all, we empower ourselves with the awareness that we don't have to live with discontent. We are connected to our lives and have the capacity to engage it fully.

5

Laying Pure Foundation

It is our light, not our darkness that most frightens us. . . . It is not in just some of us, it is in all of us. And as we let our own light shine, we unconsciously give other people permission to do the same. As we are liberated from our own fears, our presence automatically liberates others.

—Marianne Williamson, *A Return to Love*

Cultivating a warrior-spirit puts us on the path to enlightened being. We use it to make a practice of giving freely and observing a basic moral structure that guides our actions. Warrior-spirit helps us to unveil the light inside of us. We want to shine in the world in a way that lights up everything around us. When the light that each of us has in our hearts shines brightly, others see it and benefit from the example. Our sense of joy shines through and touches everyone. With enlightened being, there is no need to be afraid of anything because we will be wide open to every possibility. We will be less likely to "pick and choose" the experiences we want and do not want to have. Every moment in our lives becomes equally valuable to us. We can appreciate even the difficult moments. To paraphrase a popular saying, it really is all good. And we have to be willing to share the sense of well-being that comes from that knowledge. The difficult moments will pass just as the blissful ones do. We can't try to hold on to any of them. We let them move on so that our full attention is available to appreciate the next moment. In this moment excited, the next disappointed, after that compassionate, giving, loving. Dynamic, moving, changing, flowing. With a warrior-spirit, we get stuck nowhere, we just move with each moment as it occurs. We are completely awake, eyes wide open, fully engaged with our lives. We are able to respond to each situation that presents itself from the heart in a way that is honest and open, awake and free. That is what living is about. That is being completely alive. That is enlightened being.

A Sure Foundation

The key to having a warrior-spirit is not just an energetic presence, but also meticulous effort. Even with the Bodhisattva Vows we can't just be gung-ho and run out and expect everything to fall into place. That would be like giving someone that has been poor their whole lives a bag of gold without also giving them an understanding of the value of things. We need a reference point so that we can spend our wealth wisely. Since we commit to working with whatever tools we have to create a better life for ourselves, we have to use them to create a meaningful framework for change to take shape in. Having a solid ethical foundation helps to ensure that we feel good about everything we do in our lives.

We are very much a product of where we come from and where we have been until today, so letting go of some of the habits that hold us back takes practice. Like warriors, we have to work on the skills we will need if we want to master our lives. The framework of practice enables you to gauge yourself, to see where you stand at any given moment. For this to happen, practice has to happen in a way that is thoughtful. It won't be as meaningful to you if it is haphazard and sloppy. We have to make being awake a habit and walk on that path in a sure, steady, easy way. When you build a practice, it takes on a structure of its own and becomes supportive to you. What a great feature that is! You do something that is for your own benefit and begin to receive benefits from it right away. You build your practice, and at the same time your practice supports you in your effort to be awake in your life.

With anything you build, there has to be a strong foundation. If the foundation is not solid and firm, everything that is built on it is in danger of caving in. If the foundation is strong and later down the line some of what you build turns out to be weak, you can go back and rework just that area without starting from the beginning. So you must remember that your foundation, the starting point on which you build your practice, is critical. It's especially important to be certain of its integrity so that your practice can do its job of supporting you as you make your spiritual journey.

Any intention at all toward enlightened being has to have a foundation in moral consciousness. You cannot walk tall and master your life without morality, no matter how skillful you are in every other area. Without morality, enlightened being is not possible. Without a strong moral foundation, whatever we think we know about being compassionate and honest falls apart.

One of the biggest disappointments we have is when we place our faith in a spiritual, religious, or political leader and they betray our trust because their true moral foundation is not strong. Our leaders and role models are often compelling and appear to have the answers we need. I'm not talking about people that make mistakes in judgment and are found out before they can reflect on and correct their own mistakes. I'm talking about the people that get completely comfortable in their own magnetism, in their charisma and ability to manipulate people based on their elevated status. They don't stumble into an affair, they routinely engage in sexual relationships that feed their need for control. They embezzle money to satisfy their own greed and false belief that they should have whatever they want. Because they are magnetic, powerful, and getting lots of attention, they feel they can take what they want from life and from other individuals. They mistakenly believe that their mastery of skills entitles them to disregard other people's rights and feelings.

> *You must be the change you wish to see in the world.*
> —**Mahatma Gandhi**

Unfortunately, when we are confronted with such people we often look the other way. We do not hold them to the standards of responsibility that we must, for our own sanity and survival, hold every human being to. We are so desperate to see, know, be in contact with someone that seems to know what they're doing and where they're going in life that we excuse them for unacceptable behavior. We send them a signal that says *as long as you are entertaining us and promising us that we can become just like you, you don't have to be morally conscious in your own life.* Where is the nobility in that? What is the point of being a part-time warrior, having a part-time practice? It's a full-time job. We do this with our entertainers, athletes, senators, teachers, presidents, preachers, popes, and nuns. When we allow our leaders' behavior to go unquestioned and unexamined, it means that we don't have confidence in our own ability to use our skills. Sometimes, the failures of our straying leaders can provide us with a good reason to rely more on our individual strengths rather than look to someone else. We simply develop our own skills. We pay attention to our personal practice, and as a result, we will have the confidence and sureness that we need to both recognize morally bankrupt behavior and respond to it.

The morality that we are talking about here is not the morality that is handed down to us as a set of rules by a governing body. No institution, no government, no church or tribe needs to establish these basic moral principles, because they are absolute. When you think about it, it's very comforting. Morality relies on nothing and no one. Unlike other values, no one gets to decide whether they are "in" or not. Regardless of culture, era, or continent, there is an absolute morality that is the ultimate center of existence. It comes before anything and it cannot be altered, tainted, or destroyed. These principles are pure in the sense that they stand free and clear of any value system of the time. Because they are absolute and pure, a commitment to principles of basic morality is the strongest foundation you can build your practice on. If you really want to be strong and resilient, able to master life and not just be a paper doll, your commitment to these core, pure values is 100-percent necessary.

Commit no wrong, but good deeds do, and let thy heart be pure. All Buddhas teach this truth, which will forever endure.

—**Dhammapada**

Buddhists call these very basic moral values the Three Pure Precepts. *Precept* is a very descriptive word that helps us to really understand how we should deal with them. "Pre" means they come before anything, including our individual viewpoints that are based on what we see, hear, taste, touch, and smell. "Cepts" refers to our sense organs or means of perception. The Pure Precepts are a simple code of morality that is central to Buddhist practice, but they are not so much Buddhist values as they are basic human values. Neither Christian, Muslim, Jewish, or Buddhist at all, they are the signifiers of our basic goodness, our very deepest, original nature. The precepts are:

- to not create evil
- to practice good
- to practice good for others

They are so simple that it is easy to overlook them as unimportant, yet they are reference points for everything else. We spend so much of our time wondering how we can be at our best in the world, how we can make clear decisions about what to do and what not to do. We think *This is too obvious, there has to be something more to it.* The answer is right in front of us in plain view, but it's hard to believe that it's so simple. Instead we make two rights, a left, take a few steps forward, rest a bit, a couple steps backward and another left. Before we know it, we're lost! And the path of goodness was right in front of us all along.

. . .

WE COMMIT OURSELVES TO NOT CREATING EVIL.

We have to consciously decide that to the best of our individual ability, and out of respect for life and all the beings, animals and plants, we will live our lives in a way that doesn't bring harm to others. The decisions we make must take into account our connection to the greater community. The greatest contribution we can make to our community is to have lived harmoniously. To have been in sync with life rather than perpetuating pain. Like visiting an oasis that is beyond our imagination of beauty, we want to feel welcome in and intimate with our lives at all times. We treat our precious lives with care and we don't bring negativity to our existence. We don't want to soil it with harmful actions, thoughts, or words.

Where do these negative actions, thoughts, and words come from? How do we create evil? With the three serious poisons. Greed, anger, and ignorance are always the causes of evil. Now we see how it is all connected! The very same things that are the obstacles to enlightened being, to our being at home and at ease in our lives, are the sources of evil. Evil is not a large looming red devil with horns and a pitchfork. Quite simply, evil is being the source of pain, whether that pain is inflicted on yourself or on others. Equally damaging is thoughtless behavior. When we act without thinking, we can make careless mistakes that end up doing harm that we didn't even intend. For example, anger can have consequences far beyond the immediate situation that provoked it. It's like the dad who yells at the mom, who yells at the kid, who yells at the dog. We have to be careful of the anger we put out in the universe. Especially when we realize how each of our actions takes on a life of its own and continues to have an effect even beyond our original intention.

. . .

WE COMMIT OURSELVES TO PRACTICING GOOD.

Goodness comes naturally to all of us. It isn't something that we have to learn, but we do have to put it into practice. The urge to get up on our feet and walk tall is something that comes naturally to us as human beings. And like walking, the more you practice goodness, the more effortless it becomes. You no longer have to think "Okay, I'm going to put my left foot out heel-first, shift my weight onto my toe, now my right foot . . ." The more you practice, the easier it is to recall at all times that goodness is in your heart. It's like having money to spend that you didn't have to go out and earn. Not many things are as easy as that. Practicing goodness is not even about running out and volunteering for a cause every waking moment of your life. You don't sit there and think "What can I do that is good today?" When you do that, you attach yourself to the idea of "good" and "being good," which leads to "I am good," and soon to "I am better than others." The idea of being good can become distorted into a desire that is clung to. In this way, so-called "being good" can quickly become creating evil instead. Don't let being good become an "idea" that is artificial and outside yourself.

We need to practice goodness in a way that is based on a steady opening of our hearts and being honest with ourselves about what we see. The more aware we become of who we are, how our minds work, and how we really function in the world, the more natural the practicing of good feels to us. It is no longer something that we have to "do"; it simply becomes integrated in the way we live our lives as a result of awareness and experience. The moment we realize how connected we are to this world right now, the more obvious it becomes that there is nothing else that we can do but practice goodness. We commit to practicing good as a way of inviting awareness and compassion into our lives. With the proper invitation, goodness is sure to come.

True to the warrior-spirit, you have to honor your own intrinsic value and protect yourself, as well. Practicing good for yourself is both allowed and encouraged. Your own healthfulness and well-being is critical in your effort to master life. Taking care of yourself is a wonderful place to begin the practicing of good. You have to tend to all aspects of your well-being—physical, mental, psychic, emotional, and of course, spiritual. There is no point in going out into the world broken and unbalanced. Everything begins at home. This is not selfishness, it's common sense. Does it mean that you have to be perfect before you step out the door? No. But it does mean that looking into and tending to yourself is a necessary place to start practicing good.

Explore yourself and find the things that nourish you:

- Express your creativity regardless of whether or not you feel you are an "artist." Get paints and a brush and make art.
- Nourish and protect your body. Choose healthful foods that have been grown and produced in the best way possible.
- Stimulate your mind. Find new music that moves you.
- Pay attention to yourself. Go away for a weekend alone, or spend a day in silence.
- Revel in the magical quality of moving water. Walk on a beach or a pier or along a riverbank.
- Wake your body up, exercise your lungs. Lift light weights, run, jog, walk, or play any sport that requires you to get a little out of breath.
- Lighten your burden. Seek and ask for help when you need it or just talk out your problems with a friend, family member, or therapist.
- Share yourself. Make time for uninterrupted interaction with your family and loved ones. Spend time with them both in groups *and* one-on-one.
- Be at ease. Take ten very deep breaths, holding each for a few seconds before exhaling and relax in the arms of your lover.
- Foster intimacy. Sit face-to-face with a person you care about for at least five minutes. Without speaking, simply

look into each other's eyes, trace every line of their face. Let self-consciousness melt away.

- Honor what you love. Create an appreciation altar and adorn it with pictures of people you love, mementos and trinkets from your life, flowers, art, and objects you think are beautiful.

- Make every space sacred and worthy of attention. Make your bed every morning and clean off your desk every evening. Pay attention to the details of your life and respect order as a powerful tool.

- Use rituals to intensify your connections. Light candles and incense for no special reason. Reflect on where you are going and how you are feeling.

- Invoke the power of sound and rhythm. Repeat special sayings, poems, or sounds that feel good to you. Let these be your mantras or personal energizers.

- Build support for your spiritual practice. Find a spiritual partner, teacher, or guide whom you can talk with freely about your practice and vision of life.

- Be consistent and holistic. Make a conscious effort to practice good for each aspect of your being. Practice good for your mental, physical, emotional, psychic, and spiritual being every day you are on this earth.

If you don't learn to care for and nurture yourself, two things can happen. The obvious thing is that you will not be strong enough to deal with what life has to offer you. Even though the most painful moments in life just feel like pain when they are happening, those moments contain the greatest opportunities for growth and maturity. It's up to us to see this and take advantage of those opportunities. There are lessons in disappointment, heartbreak, and death. But if we are emotionally unstable, these events can cause us to break down or grow angry and bitter.

Rather than recognize and take away a lesson, we go forth with more pain and anguish.

The other, less obvious thing that can happen if we don't practice good for ourselves is that despite our best intentions to stop creating evil and adding to suffering in the world, if we don't feel nurtured and cared for, we can grow resentful. On the outside, everything you do seems generous and selfless. Inside, you begin to ask questions. "Why am I always the one doing everything? I am hungry too, but *I* am the only one cooking. I feel sadness but *I* am always the shoulder to cry on." This is very, very dangerous and the source of deep unhappiness. Special attention has to be paid to making sure that you feel nurtured and strong so that you do not envy other people's acceptance of the goodness that you offer to them.

In the flurry of our daily activity, taking care of yourself can easily be forgotten. You must practice good for yourself. Practice good for YOU *every single day* you are alive from this very moment forth. Do it with joy and apply every fiber of your being to it. Give it your perfect, undivided attention. In contributing to your own well-being, you give yourself agency, you foster trust and confidence in yourself. You empower yourself. You get to know who you are and gain experience in the crucial lesson of self-responsibility. If you take responsibility for your well-being, you will be able to take responsibility for all of your actions. You will be better prepared to care for, nurture, and share with your community.

This is your life. Even if there is another one after this, this is the one that you are in. It's the one that you must make the best of. Black people's history of oppression in this country has made most of us hold on to one extreme or another. We are completely self-gratifying, caught up in how much we can accumulate and benefit our individual selves. We allow our worth to be determined and our lives to be driven by our financial and material gain. Or, maybe owing to our historical experiences, we sometimes function in a blind, slavelike mode of doing for everyone to the exclusion of ourselves. We can become our own merciless masters. We have no regard for our precious lives and sacred selves.

You *are* worthy. We have to train ourselves to acknowledge our self-worth even when no one else will. You are inherently worthy. Our very existence is the mark of our sacredness. You have a responsibility to honor all that is sacred, individual You. It is the proof that we are singularly precious and uniquely valuable. Our worth cannot be taken away by anyone. Our personal, inner wealth can *not* and never will be determined by what we have. Whether we have a fat bank account or we are counting nickels and dimes in a jar, the only thing that matters is what we do with what is available to us.

Practice good for yourself first and foremost and you will be a healthier, happier human being for it.

. . .

WE COMMIT OURSELVES TO PRACTICING GOOD FOR THE SAKE OF EVERYONE ELSE.

There's not really any way that we can engage the first two pure precepts to not create evil and practice good, without the third precept falling into place behind them. Once you begin to practice good, you are already benefiting others. You become part of the solution by rejecting negativity and suffering. You contribute to greater possibilities of happiness by practicing good. So why do we have to make this separate commitment? Why hold ourselves up to the standard of this last moral value? Intention and generosity.

Intention is the seed we plant from which effort grows and action blossoms. If we don't plant and cultivate our intentions, they will never grow. Having a warrior-spirit means we are all here to make our individual, unique contribution to everyone else's ability to become enlightened beings. Only then can we truly expect to experience a world that is dramatically different from the one we know which is full of unnecessary suffering for millions of people. As you become more intimate with life, as you wake yourself up and see what is really going on, you won't be able to escape or ignore the rampant suffering. Generosity, or freely giving what we have to others, is an essential practice of warrior-spirit. To be truly generous, we have to let go of our expectations of the outcome or a return. A Buddhist teacher once said that if you give someone a gift and they immediately give it away to someone else, you should not feel angry or upset. If you do, it is likely that you haven't really "given" the gift away. If you are still holding on to it, it isn't a gift, after all.

Generosity doesn't only mean gifts and is not necessarily related to money or anything tangible. You can be generous with your time by making space to babysit for your brother's kids. You can share the extra workload with a co-worker who is swamped instead of punching out at 5:00 on the nose. Give a stranger directions. Hold the door. Pick up a fallen jacket. Spend more time with your family and less with your TV or telephone. Help out at your church. Volunteer your time. Become a mentor. And, because it does still make the world go round, it is important that you support the work and ideals you believe in with money, too. Not just when it is "easy," because we can always find ways *not* to give. We can always decide that buying a new outfit is more necessary than giving our financial support to issues we care about, but if you want there to be a cure for the many black women living with AIDS, you have to support AIDS research. If you want the mayor that has been responsible for the unnecessary loss of black men's lives to disappear into history, make a contribution to a more responsive candidate; then vote. If you want to have peace in your own life, support the effort toward peace in the whole world in any way you can.

Once you touch reality, once you know for yourself, directly experience understanding, you can never truly return to utter ignorance. No matter how long you have been ignorant, when the light is turned on, you will see what you've been missing in the darkness. Darkness is not bad, it's just darkness. It's like being asleep. Our dreams can be blissful and enticing, but we don't want to stay asleep forever. It wouldn't be considered sleep after a while, it would be a coma. The more that we try to hold on to the images that are projected on the movie screens of our minds, the harder it is to wake up out of the coma and be a part of life again. You could end up literally sleeping your life away. Without the experiences of life to help you to write new scenes and add new characters, your dream-movies will remain the same. Believe me, nothing seems quite as blissful when it's a rerun you've seen a thousand times. But if you can manage to open one eye just a little bit or concentrate and feel someone's hand holding yours, directly seeing and touching reality, you have a chance at something more. Your movie gets interrupted by, "Hey, there's something else going on out there and my projection is not the whole picture." This encourages you to explore beyond your own movie projection. Little by little, you start to wiggle your toes and blink your eyes. More of the world comes into focus and suddenly you realize that you have been asleep for a very long time. Smells come alive for you and you have the sensation of touch. You hear the power of laughter and see the intensity of the color red. Somewhere in your mind, you may miss your movie. From time to time you may remember some of the things you liked about what you projected from your mind. But given the choice, we all want to be fully awake. Being awake means you get to put your toes in cool green grass in the park and taste the salt of the ocean spray on your face at the beach. It also means you will wash dishes, lose lovers and friends, get on dreary trains and have dreary days. It's a package deal and you work with what comes in your goodie bag. Maybe life will not always be as blissful as your dream-movie projection, but it is better than going back to a mindless sleep. Ignorance is *not* an option.

The only choice you have is to work on behalf of those that cannot work for themselves. The only activities that are worthy of your time and energy are activities that serve others. The only work that is important is the work that saves our world from destruction and creates access to happiness for everyone.

There are many, many ways to serve others, and you will find a way that is most appropriate for you. You may be a firefighter that runs into burning buildings to save lives. Or, equally important, you may be a mother of four or five that tries to raise well-balanced children for the world to experience. The point is not what you do, but what your intention is in what you do. No one wants you to starve or deprive your loved ones of access to you so that you can stand on a soup-kitchen line. No matter what effort you put forth in the world toward enlightened being, it is only enlightened if it is balanced with care and regard for yourself. We have no use for a nation of martyrs. What we are creating is an endless army of energetic, compassionate warriors that understand how to use their gifts and skills to actualize and maintain a better world for themselves and for others. Awakening warriors understand that there *are* no enemies. Everyone belongs and has a right to happiness and living a life free of oppression and unnecessary suffering. We leave no one behind. Each of us goes forth in our own lives of enlightened being with the full and complete intention of bringing every single soul with us.

Bringing the Precepts to Your Life

What a relief that the foundation for our life is basic and easy to understand. We have no further need for some elaborate secret to being in the world. However, while the pure precepts are amazingly simple, they are at the same time very profound. They offer a foundation for our most difficult and seemingly impossible questions and choices about life. You can dig deeper and deeper into the precepts and you will find that they have no bottom.

You can return to the pure precepts to guide your decisions. If you ever wonder whether or not you should take a job with someone that seems a little shady, ask yourself, "Will this create evil? If I take this job, will I be working for a company or a person that adds more suffering to the world? Does their greed make them blind to the harmful effect on others? Do I want to join them and participate in someone else's pain?" Of course, if someone were to ask you, the answer to that question would always be "No, of course not." In our hearts we are good and we want to be a part of good. No one *really* wants to be "bad." So asking the question is essential. Asking yourself, checking in with what you're doing and what is really going on, is critical to maintaining your moral values. It is the only way that we can really participate in life.

When we stop questioning, we can make the mistake of adding suffering to the world. We can't accept ignorance as an excuse. Ignorance is another poison. We can't let ourselves off the hook by saying we didn't know because asking the questions, no matter how difficult, is our responsibility. Questioning is how we master the truth.

We see that we can't hide from knowing. We have to be active thinkers and truth-seekers in order to have a strong foundation. From here, we are fulfilling one of our responsible vows, the vow to master the limitless truths. This is what the work is about: seeing the connections between how we exist in the world and the effect that it has on everything else.

The Zen Peacemaker Order, part of the larger Peacemaker Community, adheres to a set of ten more precepts that I find very useful to guide me in different areas of my life.

Ten Precepts of a Zen Peacemaker

Being mindful of the interdependence of oneness and diversity, and wishing to actualize my vows, I engage in the spiritual practices of:

1. Recognizing that I am not separate from all that is. This is the precept of non-killing.
2. Being satisfied with what I have. This is the precept of non-stealing.
3. Encountering all creations with respect and dignity. This is the precept of chaste conduct.
4. Listening and speaking from the heart. This is the precept of non-lying.
5. Cultivating a mind that sees clearly. This is the precept of not being ignorant.
6. Unconditionally accepting what each moment has to offer. This is the precept of not talking about others' errors and faults.
7. Speaking what I perceive to be the truth without guilt or blame. This is the precept of not elevating oneself and blaming others.
8. Using all of the ingredients of my life. This is the precept of not being stingy.
9. Transforming suffering into wisdom. This is the precept of of not being angry.
10. Honoring my life as an instrument of peacemaking. This is the precept of not thinking ill of the three treasures.

6

Walking the
Path

Salvation is being on the right road, not having reached a destination.
—Martin Luther King, Jr.

In the Buddha's time, people believed that you were either born with the ability to achieve a greater understanding of life, or you weren't. But the Buddha said no—you don't have to be born into a special class or race. You don't have to come with special qualities. You don't have to wait for another life. Everybody has what it takes and it's within all of our grasps. We can reduce our sense of discomfort and feel at ease. We can master the art of life.

Everything you need to have a better life, you have right now. The answer to having a better life is not about getting a better life, it's just about changing how we see the one we have right now. Having been a warrior before becoming enlightened, the Buddha was all about action. So rather than relying solely on faith, he said that we can take specific steps to encourage a change in perspective. Not only that, the Buddha had the radical belief that becoming awake to one's life was possible for anyone.

The Buddha laid out eight steps that we can take toward enlightened being. He called it the Eightfold Path, and broke the steps down into three main training areas that we can focus on. Training ourselves helps us fine-tune and sharpen the skills we already have at our disposal that are necessary for living with warrior-spirit. The Eightfold Path is:

Wisdom Training
- Right Understanding
- Right Thought

Ethics Training
- Right Speech
- Right Action
- Right Livelihood

Awareness Training
- Right Effort
- Right Mindfulness
- Right Concentration

What "right" means here is true, authentic, the real deal. Not something that we make up in our minds because that is what's most comfortable or convenient. We should walk the truest path possible in our lives if we want our journey to be worthwhile and not just something that passes us by.

To stay on a path, and more important, to return to it when you get a little lost, requires the warrior-spirit of both patience and effort. Your life's transformation begins as soon as you decide you want it to. Still, we often have great expectations and want measurable progress. It isn't always easy to see how far we've come, so we have to trust the basic good intentions that come from having a strong moral foundation. When we trust ourselves because we know in our own hearts that we are good, we can practice patience with ourselves.

Being patient doesn't mean just sitting back and waiting for the life we want to come to us, either. Just like being on any other path, we have to put one foot in front of the other if we want to keep moving. We have to apply the warrior-spirit of effort. Not just here and there, but complete, meticulous effort in every moment. This kind of effort is not so that you can beat someone else to an imaginary finish line or win a prize. There's no competition and your life is not a contest. There's no reason to measure yourself against anyone. The only expectation, the only thing you ever have to do is your own personal best. Right now, in this moment, and in the next.

It doesn't matter that your best friend and her partner never seem to fight. It only matters that you make your best effort to remain open to *your* partner's perspective. Today and every day from now on. So, if you're mopping floors or typing the 97th cover letter for your résumé, mop as if you will eat from that same floor, type in preparation for your Nobel Prize. It's *your* life that you are living. Don't pick and choose when you'll be there. All of it is yours. No one else suffers more if you waste it than you. Be patient with yourself and make every effort to be fully attentive so that you don't waste any of it. That's the key to feeling and being alive. Apply patience and effort following the Eightfold Path as a guide.

Wisdom Training

Wisdom is also called insight, which means "seeing into" the nature of life. Cultivating wisdom is about bringing out the place inside you that uses direct experience and an innate sense of knowing to evaluate everything. It's like being able to see from within. Using wisdom means we no longer act out of ignorance or recklessness.

Right Understanding

The first step in wisdom training is Right Understanding. With Right Understanding, we evaluate the way we perceive everything that's happening in our world and in our lives. We look at how much of what we accept as real is based on the truth of the way things are, and how much of it is wrapped up in what we've added to it with our poisonous greed, insecurities, internal anger, and anxiety. Did the guy on the street really mean to be disrespectful by stepping on your toe, or did he simply not see you in his hurry to get where he was going? And haven't you done the same at some time? Is your mother trying to ruin your social life or is she taking care to protect the fragile innocence of your sexuality so that you can mature to be able to make informed decisions about being intimate with other people? Did your teacher or boss have it out for you, intending to sabotage your progress, or were they acting with sincere compassion by not allowing you to get away with being slack, taking the easiest way and not applying yourself?

If we want to invite true understanding into our lives, we have to be patient and think things through. We have to make an effort to stop distorting things to suit our moods and comfort levels. If we don't make an effort at understanding what is really taking place in any given situation, we'll never be able to respond to life appropriately. There is no way we can master life if we are not willing to deal with *now* just as it is, without our selfish cravings and fears latched onto it. Right Understanding is the same as The Naked Truth. That's what we have to start with in order to get to the heart of any matter.

Wisdom is not learned knowledge, it's more than that. It's deep knowing. Knowing that comes from the same center of ourselves that our goodness lives in. When we talk about wise people, we don't think about what degrees they have on their walls or how many books they've read. Some wise people are illiterate in the sense that they cannot read letters and words written on a page. They are still wise. We recognize that in them. Old women on the porches of the South that have never set foot in a classroom; African and Native American tribal elders; toothless sages in the foothills of India—they possess a wisdom beyond measure. They seem to be full of "just knowing."

Right Understanding is:
- recognizing our interconnectedness
- honoring our basic goodness
- choosing to be aware in our lives

Right Thought

To really sharpen our wisdom skills, we have to not only see and understand our life's situations in the right way, we also have to *think* of them in the right way. To have Right Thought, we have to consider matters without our stuff attached and get past all of the extra chatter that goes on in our heads. Sometimes I think of Right Thought as Clean Thought. Not clean as opposed to dirty, but clean as in pure. Without fluff. Our minds have had years and years of experience adding their own unsolicited two cents. The minute someone says something or an event takes place, we immediately begin to have a whole conversation inside our heads. And how busy it can be! Once we begin to pay attention to our minds, we quickly realize that our thoughts race around uncontrollably weaving their own tale about every little thing.

A co-worker in your office may say, "Girl, that's a really nice outfit. It looks really good on you." You think to yourself, "She never said anything about my outfit before, even when I had that blue one on that looks better. Does she really mean that? Is she just trying to be shady? Is there something wrong with my skirt?" (You might pull on it self-consciously at this point.) "Well," you think, "she shouldn't wear those stripes because they just don't look good on her. What time is it, anyway? I'm not looking forward to this meeting I have later." And on and on and on.

Did you see what happened? In the course of what we consider our normal, harmless mind chatter, we question someone's good intentions. We reveal our personal anxiety and self-consciousness about our own appearance. We entertain groundless suspicions based on self-doubt. We pass judgment on other people to deflect our own issues because this makes us feel safer than paying attention to ourselves. We hide our insecurities by focusing outside, on other people, rather than on inside. We begin to believe our thoughts just because we gave them a voice inside our heads, even though that's where they were manufactured to begin with. *Then*, right away, we cover it all up with idle chatter. It's bad enough that we give an audience to these self-perpetuated negative thoughts, but it's even worse that we don't acknowledge them. Every time we carry on harmful self-talk, we allow negativity to find a home and settle into a place in our hearts. This negative thinking is exactly what shuts us down and cuts us off, leaving us less able to be open to everyone and everything around us. And because we aren't paying attention when it happens, we don't even know how it got that way. We just wake up and find ourselves closed up and gripping tightly to all those negative thoughts.

The other part of Right Thought is the intention we put forth. Just like making vows of responsibility and committing to basic ethical values, our thoughts inform our intentions. Thoughts are like the steering wheel we turn that determines what direction we're going to go in. If we head too far in the wrong direction, we can miss the path altogether and our lives can seem more difficult. Not impossible, but very, very difficult. Thoughts are the seeds of our intentions, so they are the original source of every action we perform. Even if an action doesn't follow the thought right away, the thought will hang around until it can reveal itself in some way. Thoughts find themselves with a voice and become speech. In turn, speech eventually gives fuel to action.

Without clear, Right Thought, we allow ourselves to become defensive. We lose the sense of intimacy with our lives. We can become harsh and it becomes more difficult for us to be compassionate with others because that fuzzy thinking blurs our vision. And without the ability to think clearly, we cannot cultivate our natural wisdom and insight.

Right Thought:
- releases negative, self-serving concepts in favor of goodness
- transforms difficult moments into useful lessons
- embraces the dignity of all beings

Ethics Training

Ethics training is a lot like the pure precepts of not creating evil, doing good, and doing good for others, because it acts as a reference point for how we relate to others and how we conduct ourselves in life. If we are not skilled in engaging people through our speech and actions, we cannot possibly live in harmony with our community. What is the point of our being here, if not that? If we are unaware or unclear about how to express ourselves with our words and actions, it can be easy to mistakenly create evil or perpetuate pain and discomfort.

Right Speech

Right Speech is the natural product of Right Thought. Right Speech is about being thoughtful and aware of what comes out of your mouth. It's not just what you say, but how you say it. It is about being awake to what repercussions your words can have once they have been said. Words are very powerful. In our culture, simply because something has been said, credibility and value are given to it. Spoken words carry a sense of truth. So once words are out there, though you can apologize, there is really no such thing as "taking it back." When you practice Right Thought, Right Speech is effortless. But until Right Thought is second nature to you, you have to give Right Speech your full attention.

In Right Speech, we always honor the truth by speaking it. Even when it is difficult, unattractive, or not what someone wants to hear. Right speech is "true speech," not "pretty speech" or "easy-to-hear speech." True, honest, real. Always according to the best of your ability.

You don't beat someone down with the truth, though. In presenting and speaking truth, it's important for you to remove yourself from an expectation of or attachment to the outcome. Otherwise, truth can become a vehicle for our greed, anger, and ignorance. If you are angry and you say something that is true, but with the intent to hurt someone, you are *not* practicing Right Speech. And if you use the truth to gain something for yourself, you are still allowing the poison of greed to be a part of your life. Right Speech also means not saying harmful or negative things about other people. That doesn't mean that if you have a leader that is oppressive and abusing the rights of your community you shouldn't speak out about him or her. That would go against Right Understanding. Truth and fairness should always be your guide. When you speak out against someone or something because you truly believe they are causing harm and contributing pain to the world, that *is* Right Speech.

On the other hand, idle gossip and chatter that is about entertaining yourself and your friends is not Right Speech. Making fun of someone, even when they can't hear you, sets a chain reaction of negativity into motion that can ultimately cause someone pain. Not only is that creating evil, it does not honor our vow to take care of others.

Using words that are generally considered negative to express familiarity or affection have become a large part of black culture. *Bitch. Nigga. Boy.* Whether to greet each other or reference other people, we sometimes use these words haphazardly and without much thought. On the surface, they are just words. They seem arbitrary and should be harmless. Given the right circumstances, we use them and hear them without any immediate consequences. We understand there's no malicious intention from our friends, so it goes in one ear and out the other without our feeling threatened in the way we would if a stranger used the exact same words. It may even be funny at the time. But when we make these or any other negative words and ideas acceptable as part of our communication with one another, we invite those same words and ideas into our whole lives, without limit. We could instead choose to express our affection with words that embrace and affirm our connection to each other. And it is even more powerful to use gentle, firm language to express our disagreement and discontent. Like wise Awakening Warriors that speak deliberately, without rushing, and who take care to choose the words that clearly and concisely convey their meaning, we should not waste our words. Choose gentle, compassionate, affirming words because not only do they express your warrior-spirit and inspire others to do the same, but it's the words you speak that prepare you and form the basis for your actions.

Right Speech is:

- "How have you been, sister-friend," to your friends on the phone.
- "You are looking very well, beautiful Queen," to the sister passing you on the streetcorner.
- "Sweetheart, I love you *and* I am very angry with you. Please hear what I have to say and I will listen to you."
- "Dad, I respect your experience and perspective, but I still have to make my own decisions. I hope you can understand."

Right Action

> *Always do the right thing.*
> —*Do the Right Thing,* Spike Lee movie

Right Action is what you do with your time here. Right action is action that has good intentions at its heart and is appropriate for the situation in front of you. Our actions are how we make our intention to practice good real in our lives. It is actually doing something to save the numberless beings. It's practicing good for ourselves to support our own well-being. It's practicing good for others, serving and supporting our community. It's wholeheartedly putting into motion everything that's open, honest, and beautiful about us.

Right Action is expressing our warrior-spirit by putting it to use in our lives. It's releasing our fears, throwing caution to the wind, and baring our naked souls for everyone to see. It's taking our cultivated wisdom and making our life the working, in-process example of what our spirits aspire to.

Being Skillful

My friend Gina offers her support and guidance to her nine- and eleven-year-old nephews while their mother takes time to resolve personal issues. The boys live with their grandmother for the time being and are sometimes frustrated because it is hard for them to understand why they can't be with their mom. One day the older boy came home from school and called his aunt Gina to tell her he had been placed on pre-suspension for hitting another child in school. Instead of becoming angry and harsh with him as we often do out of frustration, Gina first listened carefully to his story—without interruption. This allowed her to understand the situation and be thoughtful about her response. She then talked to him about his stress levels and how he needed to redirect the pent-up energy that comes from feeling the kind of pressure he had been under. "Sweetheart, I know you are frustrated because things are not the way they should be. Still, you cannot hit other people. It is wrong and I know you can *feel* that it is. One of the things you can do is ride your bike after school to release some of that energy in a positive way."

Gina chose gentle, affirming words to convey an important lesson to him and guided him with skill toward a more appropriate way of being. Her nephew was relieved to be able to talk and be heard about the incident. He appreciated Gina's acknowledgment that he was suffering. Still, he understood that the way he'd reacted was wrong and felt remorseful. And, he was genuinely happy to be offered a different way to handle his stress.

We use Right Action to help our children, neighbors, and politicians see that we can live our lives in a more accepting and compassionate way. It's powerful without being oppressive, forceful without being destructive, loving without harboring selfishness.

Right Action affirms and supports the value of life. We appreciate each breath of every being, plant and animal. With warrior-spirit, in all our actions we honor the basic human right to seek happiness and decent lives for ourselves and our communities.

We practice Right Action when we:
- say good morning to the people we ride the bus with
- create loving, nurturing environments for our children to grow up in
- protect the right to happiness for all beings

Right Livelihood

Everyone needs to earn an income to feed and clothe their families. We are not monks or nuns that have taken a vow of poverty and renunciation of worldly goods, so there is nothing wrong with having a good job that provides us with comfort and conveniences. We don't have to deny the culture we live in in order to be more open and awake in our lives. Enlightened being doesn't require us to give up the way we live. It just asks us to be more aware of how we live.

Given the overwhelmingly materialistic nature of our society, if we want to be responsible at all, we have to be conscious about *how* we make our livings, too. It's important that we scrutinize what we are participating in. We need consistency throughout all areas of our lives, especially considering how many hours most of us spend in our jobs.

It wouldn't make much sense if our values, intentions, speech, and action are framed with clarity and awareness and our livelihood is out of sync. There are companies that dump toxic waste and sludge into our oceans or hide it beneath the ground in inner cities. That same ground may eventually be the site of buildings that some of our children will live in. How can we support and participate in the choking of our resources and a disregard for the health and well-being of poorer people? If we are guardians of life, we need to think twice before working for arms manufacturers that ship machine guns to dictators that commit genocide; guns that can end up on the streets of our inner cities and even in our schools. To be truly responsible, we must express our value of life with what we contribute to as much as with what we personally do and say.

It is true that many of us feel there are not many options when it comes to choosing our livelihoods. But our lives are defined by the choices we make, and some of those choices may not be easy. Making difficult choices in our lives and even sacrificing what we want in order to be responsible to ourselves and our community is warrior-spirit, too. Your choices have to be made not according to what someone else tells you, but to what truly feels right for you. What is right for me or your neighbor down the block may not apply to your life at all. Depending on your circumstances, you may have to practice patience in working in a place that you do not feel very comfortable in. If this is true, you might also have to put extra effort into changing your situation to one that is less damaging to your spirit. You would never dream of making your living at a company run by known child molesters. In the same way, you have to think of what it means to work for someone that molests whole communities and the world by tearing down rain forests that provide balance for our ecosystems and nourish life.

Part of determining what kind of work we do and what salary we accept to support ourselves is a careful examination of what we consider our needs. How much of what we "need" is really the poison greed? Or maybe competition or posturing to cover your own fears and self-doubt, which are based on ignorance? We don't need to streak around butt naked, but how many sweaters do we really need? I once read that the average American has five or six sweaters. There are children that walk around in tattered, holey jackets and shoes in the winter. Not in some far-off region of Mongolia. In St. Louis City, Kansas. In our backyards. We can't pretend to not see just because it's over our shoulders.

The norm in our culture is to accumulate more and more stuff and then pay for bigger and bigger containers in the form of houses and apartments for that stuff. If we were to really think about how many of us work extra hours to earn extra money to pay the rent that lets our five pairs of sneakers, ten pairs of jeans, numerous pants and shirts, two bikes and one unused VCR have a place to live, we might be tempted to send our *stuff* to work so we could catch a rest. Maybe you would even be tempted to release some of them. I'm not saying renounce everything you own, but deeply consider simpler living as a part of your path. Give your mind a rest from the idea that you need more. If you do make excess money (that means more than you truly need) and you do have excess stuff, put them to service in your practice of good for others. Give. Share in your fortune.

Right Livelihood:
- expresses who we are and where we want to be
- acknowledges that what we do in the world is not separate from who we are
- honors all our time as being important to our sense of wholeness and connection

Awareness Training

The last area of training is awareness. In this case, last is more like ultimate. It is awareness that is your opening into spiritual practice. Like the glimpse of light we catch from our dreamy coma that urges us to open our eyes, awareness sets us off looking for a more complete truth than the one we know. Being trained in awareness begs us to take every other step that we take toward enlightened being.

Right Effort

Right Effort speaks to both our approach to a spiritual path and our approach to our daily lives. It's a reminder to always approach our lives and pursue greater understanding with energy and vigor.

Everyone says that life is short already. What if you woke one day and realized that you really *had* been in that coma for 20, 30 or even 40 years? Since the age of two or three, you'd been in a motionless sleep, trapped in your own mind. You had never seen flowers, tasted ice cream, or held someone's hand. If you woke up with that realization, wouldn't you put every effort possible into getting to know the remainder of your life? You wouldn't waste a single moment. Every second would be delicious and savory. Your tears of pain would commingle with tears of joy from sheer delight and thankfulness that you can feel at all. You would be willing to devour the bad with the good in one hungry swallow.

If you'd been in a coma, you wouldn't waste any time if you could help it because you'd be aware of how precious and limited time is and how much had already been taken up in your deep slumber. You would keep your eyes open and give your full attention to every detail. *Those children on that swing are so happy and full of life and promise. What a miracle the vast pale blue sky of day and the endless deep blue sky of night are above us.* Every moment would count. You would squeeze every ounce you could out of life.

Well, every one of us *has* been asleep, comatose, watching those funky reruns. If we pass up the chance to get up on our own two feet and see, smell, hear, taste, and touch every experience we can, we really should just crawl back into the bed, pull the cover over our heads and disappear into an eternal sleep.

The opportunity to feel like we belong in our lives has always been available, but until we see that there's a door through which we can walk, a path on which we can travel, we may have been reluctant to move at all. Or we found ourselves spinning in circles with no direction at all. We were lost. That's okay. Every one of us has been there. The difference is, some of us are going to give up our false understanding, trade it in for reality, and put Right Effort into refining our skills of wisdom, ethics and awareness. The question is, what will you do?

With Right Effort we can:
- see that every action matters and each moment of our whole life is important
- actively commit to waking up to the lives that we live each day
- return to our path of awareness even when it does not seem clear

Right Mindfulness

Right Mindfulness is attention to detail. The step toward Right Mindfulness reminds us that we must give our complete attention to our lives—not just the parts we like or that give us pleasure—but all of it. This is, after all, awareness training. How can we be aware if we are not paying attention?

If we are mindful in every moment, the other steps on the path become easier to take. You won't be perfect. You will make mistakes. But our mistakes are even more valuable for our growth than getting it all "right." It's in the areas that are difficult for us to work with, that we make a lot of mistakes in, that we gain our greatest experiences. We learn deep truths from our most trying experiences. So if we have a tendency to be arrogant, conceited, too self-righteous, or just lazy, we have to embrace these qualities as equally important to walking the path. In fact, the only way the Buddha could possibly have figured out this path was by considering and incorporating the many mistakes he made along the way. If we put all of our effort into being mindful, we'll see a more complete picture.

Mindful. Full mind. Whatever we are working with or experiencing in this moment alone should fill our minds so that our attention can be complete. By paying full attention to our thoughts, we are able to focus and let go of the excess chatter. Our intentions are clear and thought out. When we speak, we have the presence of mind to choose our words carefully so we are less likely to hurt others with them. When mindfulness is applied to action, we find that we are more graceful and fluid because we are more certain of ourselves.

Mindfulness also expresses our sincere appreciation for the gift of life. Mindfulness transports us into the single, present moment and then into the next and the next. Without space to fret about the past or ponder the future, we end up experiencing the present moment in its complete fullness. If you ever wondered where to find it, that's where life is *always* at. In the present moment. Mindfulness brings us face-to-face with life and doesn't leave us any room for excuses or distractions. That space is where we have the chance to press right up against life and develop the intimate relationship we want to have with it. That space is where we find that the life we have been looking for is here and now. It always has been and always will be. All we have to do is be awake to it.

Mindfulness does take practice. We've really gotten used to not paying attention and being distracted, so it's a good thing that we can do anything and everything in a mindful way. When we practice Right Mindfulness, we can make our beds mindfully. We feel the sheets between our fingertips and smell the faint aroma of laundry detergent. When we shake the blanket out, we feel the air lift the tiny hairs on our arms. We immediately notice the difference between the warm, fuzzy texture of wool and the cool, tightly woven threads of cotton. We can be mindful while washing the dishes. We don't wash them to get them finished, we just wash them for the sake of washing them. It seems ridiculous to put so much emphasis on such tiny, unimportant details, but that's where your life is. Be mindful while walking up the stairs to your apartment, while waiting for the light to turn green. Any-place and anytime you want to experience the fullness of your life, all you have to do is bring your attention to this moment right now.

I always thought it was funny that Buddhists suggest practic-ing being mindful in the most mundane activities possible. It's for a good reason, though. Our daily, repetitive activities are where we really have a tendency to pass out and be completely absent. How many things do you do every day, over and over again? If you always tune out when you do those things, isn't that an in-credible waste of time? You can put it to good use by practicing mindfulness all those times. My favorite mindful activity is sweeping. I have asthma and my house gets very dusty so I need to sweep. I sweep every morning. Now, it's no longer for cleaning only, but for the opportunity to immerse myself in the activity with no distractions. I choose sweeping because I automatically get the chance to practice mindfulness over and over again.

When we practice Right Mindfulness we:
- recognize the blueness of blues and redness of reds with clarity and appreciation for their being just as they are
- can bear witness to the depths of our pain and sadness as willingly as to the heights of our joys and rapture
- are attentive to the life we are living in each moment that we are living it

Right Concentration

The last step of Awareness training is Right Concentration. Concentration is training the mind to focus like a laser on one thing and one thing only. If you've ever sat down and tried to empty your mind of thoughts and focus your attention without going on an aimless, rambling journey, you will know immediately why we need to make a practice of training our minds to focus. Right Concentration, or total concentration, is a fundamental step for being able to see things clearly.

How do we practice Right Concentration? At first, by being very, very still. Just like the warrior prince did 2,500 years ago, we touch reality in meditation. We are very fortunate that the Buddha set out on his journey and ended up plopping down into deep meditation. He gave up a lot to practice Right Concentration and get to the bottom of life. He pointed out a way for us to yank the veil off our eyes for ourselves. He taught that we can and must empower ourselves. Now we know that we don't have to wait for anyone to do it for us. But the Buddha has been dead for a long time and we can't ever gain the benefit of his experience by talking about it. We can talk and write and theorize it to death, and still we won't get one step closer. We have a good idea that his method can work because it has been passed down generation after generation for all these years. It's not the only way to enlightened being, but it is a way that works for anyone that puts patience and effort into practicing it.

With Right Concentration we:
- each take responsibility for our own freedom
- directly experience the true nature of our existence
- naturally arrive at a place of trust in ourselves and our ability to respond to circumstances

When we have a solid ethical foundation and have cultivated our understanding, thoughts, actions, and wisdom, we are better able to determine, without hesitation, what action is most appropriate in any situation. With practice, we know instinctively and from our core when to reach out to our friend that is in pain, even if they haven't said, "Please listen to me, I need your help." We know that our children's poor grades or behavior means they need our attention, not our anger. We can see that our husband or wife is tired and could use help cleaning. And beyond our immediate sphere, we are fully prepared to act when the time comes to insist that our government and institutions also act in accord with responsibility and goodness.

Awareness training may seem like it comes at the end of the Eightfold Path, but The Eightfold Path is like a circle. There are eight points on the circle to represent each of the steps. Each point is a beginning and an end. No matter where you start, you will be led to all the other points. In almost all cultures, circles represent wholeness and completion. Buddhists use an eight-spoked wheel to represent this circle of truth, or the whole truth. It's called a *Dharma* wheel. Dharma is translated as Essential Truth. If you travel each step on the Eightfold Path, you come full circle, you find truth. As promised in the Fourth Simple Truth, you can exist as an enlightened being. The Dharma wheel isn't like a bicycle wheel, it's the wheel of a ship with the spokes of the Eightfold Path providing something to hold on to firmly to steer your way through life. All of the spokes reach across the center, which is where you stand, and crisscross one another. Like everything in life, each of the steps on the path are interrelated. None of them stands alone. To take one step is to take all of them. Because the path is not a straight line, *any* step you take puts you in direct contact with them all.

7

The Profound Act of Being Still

*It was in that vast stillness that I found my sense of freedom,
an inspiration to live, to love with all my might.*

—Personal journal entry, July 1998

Left and right, everywhere you look, from billboards to TV shows to album covers, you see people striking the meditative pose.

Meditation is such a popular idea today that it's almost as sexy and magical an idea as Zen (but not quite).

If you haven't tried to meditate before, you may have decided that meditation is something like sleeping sitting up. A person who meditates is thought to be contemplative, quiet, and maybe a little wispy. The media uses images of people in meditation to convey the idea of peacefulness and bliss. The people they present are usually painfully thin. You know the look: someone sitting cross-legged, pretzel-style on the floor or perched up on a chair. Their hands may be resting on their knees with fingers forming little O's or sitting in their laps cupped into an oval. The most noticeable thing is the look on their faces.

Even with their eyes nearly closed, we can tell they are in a far-away place and wouldn't be able to hear us if we spoke to them. They look like they are floating somehow, about to rise up like a helium-filled balloon.

We see meditators in movies, on television, and on the sides of buses. They are in magazines selling pickup trucks and spa visits. They are ballerina-like ethereal women, frazzled housewives trying to soothe their nerves, fast-kicking Aikido masters like Steven Seagal, wise-looking guru-monks in flowing robes that glow Christ-like in the light of 8,000 surrounding candles, and let's not forget the occasional sophisticated, super-healthy, grounded guy that drinks lots of protein shakes, carrot juice, and green stuff.

One of the things that makes meditation so confusing is that there are so many types and traditions, and they all have different goals. People meditate to relax, to get their minds off problems, to improve their health, to strengthen their bodies, to connect with spirits, to visualize what they want to achieve in their lives, to develop psychic abilities, and sometimes to levitate or walk on fire. The instructions for just how to achieve a specific goal are as varied as the aims.

Relaxation and improved health are far and away the most popularly presented benefits of meditation. While these are very helpful, they are not the primary intention of the meditation practice of Zen.

Zen Meditation

Zen Buddhism has meditation as its most central characteristic. "Zen" is the shortened version of *zenna*, a Japanese translation of the Chinese word *ch'an*. Each of these words is a reading of the Sanskrit *dhyana*, which means (surprise!) meditation. And while pop culture has given Zen different hazy mystical readings such as "coolness, nonchalance, spareness," or anything Asian, its real meaning is plain and simple meditation. The Chinese Ch'an and Japanese Zen schools of Buddhist tradition are considered the meditation schools.

The meditation practiced in Zen communities all over the world in many countries, many languages, is called *zazen*. *Za* means seated or sitting. So we are practicing sitting meditation or just plain "sitting." Just like the Buddha did under a tree for six years. He just sat there.

On the outside, that's what it looks like, just sitting. It seems too simple to be of any value. Don't be fooled; what happens over time in zazen can be so deep, so profound and yet so subtle, that it changes the way you see everything. Meditation is the method that you use to find space and freedom. With practice, meditation reveals the spaciousness and calm that is inside you. It is from that place that your perception of the world is dramatically and irreversibly altered. Because your mind becomes less cluttered and you are not tripping over your desires, you can walk with ease. It is from here that you can live your life with grace.

Zen meditation practice is about developing single-pointed awareness. The reason that we want to develop total concentration and awareness is to understand how our minds work. Once we understand how the mind works, we will see reality, we will know the nature of all things. That insight, the inner knowing that comes from having experienced it for ourselves, is the final key to mastering life.

A person that has touched reality and is truly intimate with their world is a thing of glory. Their presence is radiant and unintrusive. Their very being is enlightened. They are vibrant and perpetually present. It is clear that they are not ruffled and upset by life's events. This is called equanimity. It is a quality that is the product of insight. The calm that emanates from them is a sure sign of their appreciation and mastery of life. They are the warriors that have found their way home. We only have to follow in their footsteps.

It may help to know that meditation is not magic in the sense of hocus-pocus. (If any of you actually levitate, please let me know right away!) The change that occurs in your perception when you develop your ability to concentrate is based on a change in the way you are using your brain. The part of our brain that our culture focuses on the most is the intellectual part. Our society places a very high value on increasing our intellectual capacity or "being smart." Almost all schooling is intended to develop the intellect. Intellect is the domain of the frontal part of our brain. Even when we think of "where" our minds are, we point to our foreheads, in the front.

So the rest of the brain doesn't feel like it belongs to "mind" at all. Really, it doesn't. We initially receive every bit of information from the outside world through the five perception tools or sensory organs. Our eyes see, ears hear, noses smell, tongues taste, and bodies feel. After we receive the information from our senses, mind finally organizes and applies labels based on everything else it has stored.

We call the reception of information through our sense organs "sensation." But we quickly go to our brains to try to classify it or form concepts. Concepts are based on what we have already taken in and stored in our memories. Whether formally or informally, this comes from what we have learned. Our concepts come from lectures from a teacher or boss, from what our mommas told us or grandfathers showed us with a swat on the behind, from a scare we got, from nasty things people have said to us or we have heard in passing, or even from the constant flow of media that we are exposed to. While this can be useful for navigating the world sometimes, it is the concepts we form that also keep us from seeing things *now* as they are.

The area of the brain that allows us to experience things in their original form, free from our learned concepts, is right down in the middle of the brain. It's called the thalamus. The thalamus is responsible for the other type of brain activity we have, our instinct.

Instinct is the very first thing that signals us to take our hands out of the fire, even before we are able to relate fire to the idea of hot. We don't stop and formulate an idea before we act, we just act instinctively. But instinct isn't limited to shielding us from danger. Nor is it just reactionary. Our instincts access a knowing that we never learned. It gets at primal knowledge or "first knowing." It's the knowing that you experienced before you knew anything, and it is where all other knowing begins. It is original. A knowing such as that, that is beyond our intellectual comprehension and is not based on anything we have been fed externally, must come to us even before we were born. It is our most original nature. It has nothing to do with age, culture, time, place, race, sex, or IQ. Since we know that at least on a day-to-day basis instinct originates from inside our brains, it is truly knowing from within.

Our instinct operates all the time and has a lot to do with what moves us to seek out things to nourish our spirits, like beauty and love. But for the most part our original nature arises and acts on our behalf without us having anything to do with it. It is random at best, so we are not able to experience the full power of it. If meditation practice is about trying to get at our original knowing to find a place of freedom and a place without fear, we have to train ourselves to be able to gain access to our original nature at will. It can be scary to imagine tapping into your instinctively original nature. You may feel your instincts will run wild with desires, fears, anger, and other feelings. Yet if we take on our original nature instinctively within our awakened warrior-spirit, we take on fundamental and deepest wisdom. We cannot control our instincts, and attempting to will only result in a huge sense of failure. Control is just as much a concept created in the mind as anything else is. What we can do is create the best conditions possible for instinct to function uninhibited, and let the by-product, insight, simply arise. Each time we sit down to meditate we are inviting wisdom into our lives.

As with everything else, in order to create the best conditions for meditation, we need to create a good foundation. For practicing meditation, or sitting, we find that foundation in posture. Since you start your meditation sitting down, without good posture your foundation is weak. And as we know, anything that is built on a weak foundation can come crashing down. With sitting, if you lack good posture, you lack the best conditions for concentration.

When it comes to our physical bodies, the thing that always gets in the way of our concentration and provides us with lots and lots of material to be distracted by is pain. Yes, there it is. You should know this up front. When you first begin to sit, you may and probably will experience some physical discomfort. The pain is in our shoulders, neck, back, knees, and hips, among other places. My ankles still give me grief. Hopefully, if you do your best to pay close attention to your posture, you can eliminate most, if not all, of the physical discomfort. Unless you have a specific injury, like my ankle, the pain usually comes from a buildup of tension in the muscles. That tension occurs because our bodies naturally try to balance themselves out. So if you sit lopsided, letting your head lean to the left, the muscles in the right side of your neck pull back trying to get themselves right. (They do it by instinct!) Since our muscle tissue is all connected, our shoulders and backs get in on the pulling, too. You're sitting there with all the tension building up and, depending on your tolerance level, your body suddenly says, "Enough!" and you experience good old-fashioned pain.

Pain and physical discomfort happen to be the source of countless distractions. Pain has a very big mouth and when it calls our attention, our minds tend to it almost automatically. Instantly, we are distracted by this call and the tending to the call. And there goes our concentration. So let's start our practice of meditation by building a solid foundation.

Practicing Your Posture

Here are the most effective postures with their names and a brief explanation of how to do them. They are here in the order of what is traditionally considered the most balanced. The first few require some flexibility, so be sure to go through them each and choose a posture that you feel comfortable with.

Full Lotus

The infamous full-lotus position is the pretzel look we associate with meditation. It is considered the optimum posture for developing concentration because it puts us in full contact with the ground and, when mastered, is absolutely balanced. The left ankle crosses over and rests on the right thigh. The right ankle does the same on the left thigh. The rest of the instruction pretty much applies to all the positions unless otherwise noted. When you put a small cushion, rolled-up pillow, or towel under your butt, both your knees will end up planted on the floor. The cushion should usually be about three or four inches thick, but it's best to find the height that makes you most comfortable. The buttocks are firmly planted and the spinal cord in the back is straight up and down, not swaying to the left or right. It is also helpful to put your cushion on a mat or folded-up blanket to rest your knees on and protect them from the hard floor beneath you.

The very top and center of your head should be stretched toward the sky as if someone had you on a string and were pulling it up. While being pulled up, pull your chin in somewhat close to your chest. Align your shoulders with your ears. Check to make sure that your head is not tipped forward or backward, left or right. After being sure that you are aligned in just this way, take a DEEP breath and relax. Don't slouch. Just relax.

Half Lotus

The half-lotus position is a little easier to get into. Basically, instead of putting both ankles up on your thighs, you put one ankle up on your thigh and let the other foot rest underneath the opposite thigh. Be careful not to sit on your foot with your full body weight because it'll go to sleep quickly. Your head, back, hands, and eyes all do the same thing as in full lotus.

An important thing to remember about half lotus is that it is asymmetrical and finding balance in it takes a little more effort. You can end up leaning in one direction or the other, so you have to pay more attention to aligning yourself correctly. This position is good for people who find that they are flexible enough for full lotus, but may have a little stiffness in one knee or one ankle that makes full lotus uncomfortable. It can help you increase your flexibility. In one sitting you can put the left ankle on the right thigh; the next time, do the opposite. Over time, your flexibility will increase. If you find yourself unable to sit this way for five full minutes without discomfort, try the next position.

Burmese position (Cross-legged)

The Burmese position is what most of us call "sitting cross-legged." Both of your feet lie flat on the mat or blanket beneath you. It is a very well-balanced posture and good for people who don't have too much trouble with their knees. It's important to remember to push your belly forward and thrust your buttocks backward to keep the right curve in your spine and not end up rounding the spine (which will cause you to build up tension).

Seiza position (Kneeling)

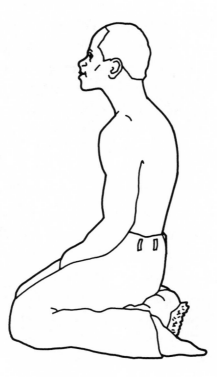

Seiza (pronounced "say-za") is a kneeling position that takes a lot of pressure off the knees and moves it more to the base of the spine. It's probably the position most widely used for people just starting meditation who often find sitting in any cross-legged position hard on their knees. In seiza, you get on your knees and put your cushion between your legs. Settle down with your buttocks on the cushion, letting your weight rest on your butt. All of the same things apply for the rest of your body. Seiza is very helpful for learning how to put the right emphasis on your abdomen. Many times, people sit on a small seiza bench made especially for meditation. This is very helpful for relieving pressure on your knees.

Last, but no less valid, is the position used when sitting in a chair. Some of us may simply not be flexible enough to sit on the floor, and will find it too painful. The point of meditation is to develop concentration, not to put ourselves through excruciating pain. While there are benefits to sitting on the floor and being in contact with the ground, more important than attaching to any ideas about which position is "best" is actually doing the meditation. If a chair is where you find that you are able to practice, then practice in a chair. Sitting in a chair is very helpful for people who are not flexible, have had knee injuries, have poor circulation, or just need a change from the floor positions. During extended meditation periods, many people change up and sit in a chair for a while just to give their knees and ankles a rest. No matter what your level of flexibility, everyone should learn to meditate in a chair so that their practice can be done anywhere. When you can meditate in a chair you can do it on the train on the way to work, while waiting for a doctor's appointment, in the park during winter, or after a rain when sitting on the ground is not very functional.

In your chair, push your shoulders and butt back so you don't hunch, and plant your two feet firmly on the ground. Don't cross your legs or feet on top of each other. You want to achieve the same three-point stability as in any other posture.

Checking Your Posture

The best way to make sure your posture is okay is to take off your top and practice sitting in the mirror. With a shirt on, it's harder to see what your shoulders and back are doing, so check without one on. Your back has the strongest muscles in your body and can pull everything else out of sync, so pay special attention to it. Alignment is key. Then turn to the side to check your ears and shoulder alignments. Remembering to keep them aligned helps keep your head where it belongs. This may not seem comfortable at first because so many of us are used to keeping our heads thrust forward or pulled back. Rely on what looks right, not what feels right. Line up your shoulders with your ears and make sure your chin is tucked in. Last, turn toward your front and double-check everything. If you took care with your rear and side view, it should all look okay.

Hands

Now for your hands. Place your left hand in your right hand, lining up the knuckles. Let the tips of the thumbs touch very lightly. Imagine holding a very thin sheet of paper between them. That is all the pressure you need. Your hands should form a small oval. They then rest on the heels of your feet (your lap in the Full Lotus). This little oval should end up right at your abdomen. Your thumbs will be about an inch or so below your navel. You have formed the cosmic *mudra*. A mudra is a gesture made with your hands that evokes a particular idea or energy. This way of holding your hands during meditation goes back thousands of years. It directs and concentrates your energy in the abdominal area. Specifically, a spot about three inches below your navel called the *tanden*.

Mouth

Next, swallow all your saliva and put your teeth together, but don't clench your jaw. Now place the tip of your tongue against the roof of your mouth, just behind your two front teeth. This keeps you from swallowing a lot, because even that can become a distraction when you are very quiet and still.

Eyes

The last thing is what you do with your eyes. There seems to be an unspoken rule that meditating means closing your eyes, and people do it automatically. That's a quick road to falling asleep! In zazen, your eyes are not closed. Instead, you lower your eyelids about three-fourths of the way. Fix your attention on one single point on the wall or floor in front of you. Relax your eyes, letting them go out of focus and blur a little so that you are not staring at one spot, but more like looking past it. This helps you to keep your mind from wandering. It's also a helpful way of recognizing that you have become distracted because you'll suddenly realize that instead of the spot on the floor, you are now looking at your knee, or out the window, or you've just wandered off to the right. Bringing your attention back to the spot helps to put you back on track again.

Following the Breath, Stilling the Mind

Once you've practiced your posture, you can begin the actual practice of meditation. To quiet our minds down, we focus on something that comes natural to us. This way, we don't introduce thinking. Since thinking is just the thing that creates distractions, we don't want to intentionally add it in.

More than anything else we do, breathing comes completely naturally to us. It unifies our external, physical selves with our internal selves. Ever since we were slapped on our bottoms and took in our first deep breath of air, we've been keeping ourselves alive by breathing. We never really think about our breath until it is abnormal for some reason. When we have run hard or are not feeling well, our breath suddenly draws our attention. For a little while, we become reacquainted with the relationship between our breath and our lives. As a function of our bodies, breathing is life-sustaining, precious, original. No one tells us how to do it. Most of the time, breath stays in the background, not demanding our attention at all. In meditation, we use this original nature of the body to unify us with the original nature of our mind. We close the gap between perception and action. We eliminate everything we can that separates us from being completely aware of ourselves. In other words, we focus our attention on the most natural function of our bodies, in order to get our wandering, thinking, noisy minds to stop running all over the place; in order to get to the most natural state of our mind. We unify the body with the mind.

The funny thing is that as naturally as breathing comes to us, when we first try to pay attention to it, it is hard to keep our focus on it without trying to control it. That says a lot about the way we are on a daily basis. Just as our minds attach concepts and history to each sensation that comes to us through our senses, we try to manipulate the breath when we purposely pay attention to it. It's hard for us to just leave well enough alone and let things be as they are.

Try this two-minute exercise. Sitting or standing wherever you are, count to ten using your inhalations and exhalations as a guide. On your first inhalation, count "one." Then exhale and count "two." Next inhalation, count "three," and so on until you get to ten. Then start over again. Focus your attention completely on the path that air travels into your body, through your nostrils, down into and filling your lungs, causing your chest and belly to expand and fill. Then follow the breath out again up through your chest and out of your nostrils or mouth. Your attention should be so focused on your breath that there is no room for any other thoughts. Whenever you do find yourself thinking of anything other than just counting your breaths, begin the count over again. So if on in-breath ONE, out-breath TWO, in-breath THREE, my ear is itching . . . oops! Start again. In-breath ONE, out-breath TWO.

Here you are with a pretty simple set of instructions. So simple, really, that a small child can do it. Everyone breathes, right? You've been doing it all your life, so it's that easy. You just have to pay attention to breathing. Other than that, all you have to do is count to ten and then start over again at one. Simple. There's no one in your head with you and it's not a test, so be completely honest with yourself and be sure to begin your count again the moment you find your mind wandering at all. Not so easy. One of the first things that we notice in meditation is how little control we have of ourselves. Whatever your experience, and whether this is your very first try or your tenth year meditating, all of us find it difficult to keep our minds still even doing something as simple as counting and as natural as breathing.

If you tried the sitting meditation just now, on reflection, you may realize that in those moments when you were just counting your breath you felt completely still. Nothing else happening. Just you and your breath. Very still. In that stillness, everything else seems to disappear into the background and there is only you left. It becomes very quiet without all the noise our thoughts make in our heads. We experience a still mind. It may have been a fleeting moment, but there you were. Your mind stopped calculating, classifying, and organizing everything it perceived. Without your thoughts intruding on every single thing, you were left with the clarity of pure perception. When our perceptions are no longer dressed up or boxed in by our endless list of ideas, we can understand what is meant by "seeing things as they are." When we are very, very still in the way that meditation allows us to be, we can find the space to let everything be as it is.

It is from that space that you will find the room you need to see who you are and how you fit in the world.

Until you have your own personal and direct experience of how meditation reveals your original nature, you're going on faith. And while faith is okay as a diving board to leap into spiritual seeking, nothing you hear will ever *really* satisfy you and touch you deeply in your heart until true awareness is your own. Any path toward enlightened being in the world that does not ask you to make the experience your own is asking you to stretch too far. This path not only encourages but demands that you make the experience your own.

Meditation is the foundation that converts principles into firsthand experience. It transforms ideas into lived reality. There is no replacement for it. The understanding and clarity of pure perception doesn't happen overnight. And yes, it does require commitment, effort, and practice. But it costs you nothing but a little bit of time. The return, on the other hand, is immeasurable, and the value of direct, personal understanding can never be overstated.

living
every day
with
fearlessness
and grace

8

Lovingkindness: Discovering Compassion

Lovingkindness is like true friendliness. Not fake, smile-in-your-face, cheesy friendliness. And definitely not the kind that's about accepting anything anyone decides to lay on us. It's the real kind that allows you to accept as they are, including the bumps and warts. You are open to people so that you can gently accept everything that comes up about them, including the things you didn't always know. What we are not usually taught is that we have to cultivate that kind of loving acceptance of our own selves before we can really accept anyone else. You have to open your heart to who you are, with both your strengths and flaws and recognize that you are a complete and perfect being, too.

Curiosity Brings You Back

In order to see lovingkindness in action, we have to be curious about the lives we have in front of us. We spend a lot of time looking for "something new" that will make us feel alive and in touch with ourselves. It could be a new boyfriend, new shoes, new whatever. One of the things that happens to us when we get so fixated on finding that new thing is that we forget about what's already there. Flowers are as beautiful when they are alongside the highway as when they are in a glass vase delivered to our door. There's definitely nothing wrong with getting great pleasure out of the ones that arrive with a card and a sentiment attached, but still, if we look around us, we can appreciate the roadside ones and not just forget about them. We have to do that with ourselves as well. You can practice curiosity right now by being really honest and exploring why you're interested in spiritual ideas. Think about why you picked up this book or why you go to church every Sunday, even when you don't feel like it. Look at the reasons closely. Invite them into your mind and make them feel welcome. Then be curious enough to ask yourself questions:

- Do you feel lost or in pain and feel perhaps that a spiritual teacher or book will have the answer?
- Do you want to be a better person, perhaps to see yourself as a "good" person, and hope you'll learn how?
- Are you here because you want to be better than other people, seem more earthy and in touch than they are?
- Are you here because Zen is trendy these days?
- Is this one of many paths you've explored and just as quickly dropped when something else caught your attention?
- Have you given up on the faith you were raised with and are searching for anything but that?
- Are you just plain sick of the racism, bigotry, violence and poverty you see, and do you want some relief?
- Did you like the book cover and just think it's cool to be seen with and will make you appear smart, or even more spiritual?

What *do* you want from your spiritual practice? That's a good reason to be here. Which one? All of them, because no answer matters in the end. No one takes up a spiritual practice for the "right" reason, because there isn't one. Whether you are the reincarnation of a saint, born time and time again to relieve others' suffering, or a sister or brother trying to hold your own family together, your reason for pursuing a practice is equally valid, equally honorable. Any and every reason for arriving on your spiritual path is the best reason you could possibly have.

Self-acceptance:
Being Gentle with Yourself

As a country and as a community, we spend a lot of time talking about the fact that we have got to get over our differences. This is certainly true, but too often we are not being taught how. The truth is that as long as we are looking for the answer to resolving our differences with "others" on the outside, we will not find it. If we continue to look in books, seminars, conferences, or eight-tape audiocassette courses, we will continue to find new reasons to look over our shoulders and squint our eyes in mistrust at the first person, group, or idea that doesn't fit into the mold that we are expecting. If we are being directed toward something that lies outside ourselves, we are not being pointed in the right direction. We're just looking for the right answers in the wrong places.

Whatever your doubts and beliefs about who you are, you have to learn how to be at ease and make friends with yourself before you can truly be at ease with the rest of the world. This is one of the most profound benefits that introspection or looking inward has to offer. Meditation reveals that the obvious place to begin is not in some *other* place, it's right here. The person that you need to learn to get along with first, to make peace with before anyone else, is you. Who you most need to honor, nurture and embrace *exactly* as he or she comes, is you. Self-acceptance doesn't mean there isn't room for improvement, but it does mean that while you're working toward that improvement, you allow yourself room to breathe. You allow room for the missteps on your path, and that allows you to learn from *all* of your experiences rather than quickly discarding the "bad" ones as screw-ups that have gotten in the way of your goal.

There is no part of yourself that should be rejected. But it's not as easy as looking in the mirror and saying, "I love me. I love me just as I am no matter what anyone says." Even if that works for a little while, it probably won't last. The process of learning to be gentle with and accepting of yourself is gradual but more than worth the effort. It's like finding an amazing, beautiful, and valuable work of art that over time has been covered with many, many layers of dirt and grime. In order to recover this precious treasure without damaging it, you have to gently rub away the grime. Slowly, methodically, with patience. You may have to put it down for a while and return to it. But with a continued effort, it can be done.

Warrior-spirit is not about closing yourself in and being guarded at all. On the contrary, true warrior-spirit means being as open as possible. It's making a practice of being open. Practicing being intimate, getting close. Not just to the people that you already feel love for and want to be close to, but to everyone. Open to the dentist, the bus driver, the clerk. Little by little you open up more and more. Open to Republicans if you're a Democrat. To the Liberals if you're Conservative. Your capacity to appreciate difference deepens. Open to white folks, Asians, Latinos, and East Indians. You accept the whole world with open arms not because you have been told you should, but because you realize in your heart that we are all ultimately deserving of love and compassion. Open to the poor and homeless, the sick and dying.

There's no magic involved here, and it isn't nearly as impossible or distant as it may sound. The way to get to this place of openness and compassion is to practice opening more and more to yourself. *All* of yourself. The rough, unrefined parts as well as the areas you are proud of and like to recognize. The practice of meditation helps us call on the gentle "watcher" inside us who views all the contradictions that make us who we are without judging any of it. When you are sitting there counting your breath and a thought comes up, acknowledge it for just what it is . . . a thought. Even better, notice the thought and name it exactly that. So if you find yourself thinking that there's no way you are going to be able to sit still for five minutes, name the thought. "I'm having a thought that I won't be able to sit here." Okay, that thought can move on. Your knee begins to ache a little. "I'm having a thought that my knee hurts." Perfect. Next you remember how Yvette really got on your nerves last week. "I'm having a thought that Yvette pisses me off." That's okay, too.

There are no good thoughts or bad thoughts. When you name them like that, they all end up just the same. Thoughts. The steam is taken out of the hot and fiery ones. The lazy ones perk up because they are being noticed. Each of your thoughts gets a name and is then allowed to move on. Without all the drama you would normally dress them up in, they are just naked thoughts. Through meditation, every bit of us gets to be seen and acknowledged, rather than forced into a corner. We gain our sense of wholeness from that self-acceptance.

Of course, there will be days when it will seem impossible that you could be anything else but the wretched, confused person you secretly believe you are. It will seem even more impossible, as it sometimes still does to me, that you can start to be okay yourself simply by spending some time and paying attention to your breath and being still. That doesn't mean we want to ignore our thoughts. That's a sure way to make them stay right there in front of you. Your thoughts have spent their whole lives being entertained. They are accustomed to appearing out of nowhere and having you go along for the ride. Sometimes they are important indicators of what is going on inside you. They hint at things that you may be avoiding or just not giving enough attention to. Either way, trying to just ignore your thoughts is self-repression. Lovingkindness teaches us to accept everything that is.

When you do have thoughts that are calling attention to deep feelings that are in need of being recognized, it's better to acknowledge them. Let yourself become so friendly with even the most painful feelings that you can sit side-by-side in silence with them. Don't talk about your feelings or try to figure them out in your head, just sit quietly and look deeply into them so that they can be accepted and embraced without being pushed down or beaten back.

Childhood Memories

Years ago, my father moved us to the Flatbush section of Brooklyn from Lefrak City in Queens where I'd grown up. Like many urban children, I was a "latch-key" kid. School let out at 3:00 P.M. and neither my dad nor my stepmother would get home until at least 6:30, so I'd come home and let myself into the house every afternoon. This new building we moved into had a doorman that greeted everyone as they came and went. Santiago was an older man—at least 50, though at that time it wasn't easy to say. He was friendly and very helpful, always offering to carry heavy grocery bags or to mind packages that arrived throughout the day. I spent lots of afternoons hanging out in front of the building talking to him when there weren't any other kids around.

He wasn't the superintendent, but he had the key that unlocked the elevator so that I could go to the basement where the building's laundry room was. It wasn't always locked, but sometimes I'd have to ask him to open it if I needed to throw some clothes in the dryer. There were a few times when Santiago rode down in the elevator with me. He'd disappear around a dark corner that led to the other side of the large building to look at meters or perform some other unknown task. One of those times, he reappeared and stood talking while I finished loading the dryer. In what now seems like a bizarre turn of events in a fitful dream, he was close, pressing me up against the cold, dank basement wall. I remember him sweating as he fumbled in his pocket and with his pants zipper, even though it was cool down there. The nice doorman squeezed a crumpled ten-dollar bill into one of my hands and his penis into the other.

I don't remember how many times I visited the basement with Santiago or even why. As an adult, I can still feel the sense of loneliness and abandonment that had become a part of my life once my father had my new stepmother, sister, and new baby brother to give attention to and he and I were no longer as close as we had been. And for years, the memory of the sweat beaded on Santiago's forehead was too much for me to recall. But all that time I carried with me a deep sense of guilt, because I'd allowed those meetings to take place even though I knew I didn't want to be there. I felt that I was somehow responsible for inviting him and if I had done things differently, it never would have happened.

That dark secret and all of the feelings that came with it buried themselves deep in my spirit and I was content to leave them there because they were too painful even to acknowledge. But seventeen years later, as I sat meditating, these images began to take form in my mind. I'd pushed them back so far for so long that they seemed completely foreign to me and, initially, I didn't even recognize the experience as my own. After trying to shift my attention away from it again and again with no luck, I "watched" the story that was demanding attention unfold. I observed the entire scene without rushing to classify what was going on. Safe from the accusations and judgment, the young girl that I had been then stepped out from the shadows of my mind and shared her fear and confusion with me. I witnessed her suffering as she tried to make sense of something that was senseless. I stood face-to-face with the guilt that she took with her everywhere from that moment on. When I acknowledged her experience without judging her, she was no longer condemned to hide and carry the burden of her pain alone. She could come out and be okay because I gently accepted her and allowed *that* me to be part of me, too. And as the images came, took form, were seen, and left, one sentence that I'd never been quiet enough to hear before repeated itself. It was just a whisper at first because it was coming from a place that I didn't usually know how to listen to. But the quieter my mind was, the louder the voice, until I could hear it so clearly I knew it had always been there. "You were only ten. You were only ten. YOU WERE ONLY TEN." Finally, my ten-year-old self was free.

It is very hard to face our embarrassment, guilt, fears, hidden hopes, and unmet expectations. But when we return to stillness over and over again and all of our garbage begins to reveal itself, we have no other choice but to look right at it with our eyes wide open. After we've run ourselves ragged with excuses and stories, after we've run and hidden and then returned sheepishly, feeling embarrassed, we may get to feeling helpless, miserable, angry, shameful, self-loathing. It can be very difficult to sit there and recognize those feelings. But it happens to all of us in some form or another. We come face-to-face with ourselves and don't like what we see. Our habit of avoiding suffering makes us use anything we can to get away from it as fast as possible. It's returning that's important. Once you've taken off the thick suit of armor, passed through the barriers, and peeled back the layers and layers of conditioning, you find a place that is raw and exposed like an open wound. What is amazing is that right there, at the most tender of places, is the spot. This is where the beginning of our transformation lies. When we embrace our whole selves, we arrive at the door of opportunity.

The opportunity is to be greeted with the great big, wide-open arms of acceptance. Acceptance for who we are, just as we are, whatever that may be: funky attitude, arrogant, self-pitying, too fat, kinky-haired, pimpled, freckled, too tall, too short, not enough money, always late, high-strung, unmotivated, skinny as a rail, high yellow, chinky-eyed, Kunta Kinte–looking, half-breed, flat-nosed, dim-witted, still living with your momma, working at McDonald's, conceited, know you better than anyone else, Cuchifrita, Coconut, Spic, Negro. There is an infinitely brilliant, fully enlightened, unfathomably excellent, perfect being waiting at the door. Waiting to take you in even though you are all those things and ten thousand more. So say to yourself, "Here I am, in the best way I can be at this moment." And that is all that should ever count.

Compassion: Essential Warrior-Spirit

Lovingkindness is wide-open acceptance of someone just as he or she is. It's learning to give of ourselves without expecting anything in return. Armed with the open mind and open heart that come from self-intimacy and self-acceptance, you can begin the very possible task of truly accepting others. When you practice accepting yourself in your many different forms and moods, you naturally develop an ability to see your own self in other people.

As you learn how to accept yourself, you learn how to accept them. That's the true meaning of compassion.

Love and compassion are at the core of our warrior-spirit. They are our most essential tools. Compassion is about opening yourself to other people's suffering. You don't take on the pain and get bogged down by it. You become a witness to the sameness of your experiences, the universal nature of our existence. You learn to acknowledge suffering, without having to turn away from it because it makes you uncomfortable. You bear witness to the pain so that healing can begin. Compassion is the thread that connects the hearts of all human beings to one another. When you really recognize other people's pain, you feel compelled to take action in response. It is impossible not to.

Depending on the situation, that response could be to offer a hot meal, to take to the streets and protest, to put your arms around someone, or just to sit in quiet recognition of their pain. The point is that the warrior-spirit of compassion takes action. True love cannot help but respond. With warrior-spirit, we respond from the deepest place in us, that knows no judgment. We respond because we *feel* what others are feeling. We respond out of our appreciation of and intimacy with our humanness. Each of us experiences our lives in our own way, but we agree in our hearts to live with the awareness of other beings that expresses our basic goodness. Without awareness and compassion, it will be impossible for all of us that live on this planet together to get along. Getting along with people is as simple as making room in our hearts and minds to allow them to be as they are without anyone feeling threatened. As long as there are different people in the world, there will be different opinions and perspectives. The only way to get along is to begin from a place of acceptance.

Compassion seems like a nice buzzword, and we all want to have it. But compassion isn't an idea that can be taught. You can't pick it up at the bookstore. Compassion has to be felt. It's one of those things that reveals itself without your having realized that it was at your disposal all along. You can't manufacture what was always there, but you can create the condition in which it is most likely to thrive.

In the very heart of our most "negative" feelings, there lies an overflowing source of openness, acceptance, and generosity to ourselves and others. Developing our skills of compassion teaches us to be open so that we can resolve differences in a balanced and meaningful way. Recognizing our own selves in everyone else, we can let go of our rigid expectations of our children. Instead of living from a place of judgment, we extend our ability to accept ourselves to our mothers and fathers, realizing from the heart that we all have self-awakening to do.

The expression of lovingkindness and compassion resonates deeply for all of us and encourages us to open our hearts. Our compassion embraces the humanity of all beings and our lovingkindness accepts what comes, without the harsh glare of judgment. We need them both to speak the language that every human needs in order to grow. When we live with compassion, we step beyond our limited selves into the wide-open spaciousness that is love.

9

Mindfulness: Grace and Seeing Things As They Are

It's a matter of responding in an improvisational, undogmatic, creative way to circumstances, in such a way that people still survive and thrive.

—Cornel West, **Breaking Bread**

A few years ago, I went to an event at a big church in New York City that has become famous for the diversity of its guests and presentations. This particular night they were hosting *An Evening With Thich Nhat Hanh,* who is a much-loved Vietnamese Buddhist monk, poet, and teacher. Nhat Hanh is well-known for organizing peaceful protests and speaking out against violence, and his activities have resulted in his living in exile in France ever since the Vietnam War. He advocates for peaceful resistance and was nominated by Dr. Martin Luther King, Jr., for the 1968 Nobel Peace Prize. Thây, as he is affectionately known, speaks a lot about the way in which love can function to heal us and open our hearts to one another. In particular, he talks about the practice of mindfulness as a tool for being aware of our lives and what goes on around us.

His teaching style is deceptively simple and goes straight to the heart. Because of that, Thây has developed a very large following in America and people line up to hear him whenever he comes to speak. This night was no exception. There were literally people lined up around the corner to get into the event which, even though the church was very large, was standing-room-only. People were moving back and forth trying to get to their seats or find a comfortable place in which to stand or sit on the floor for the next two hours. My companion and I were lucky enough to find seats, and we sat talking to each other as the program was about to begin.

The evening started off with a woman playing guitar and singing a song about peace and love. Then Thây was introduced by the pastor of the church. Even with the huge number of people in the cavernous space, the room fell into a hushed silence of anticipation. But Thây didn't begin to speak. There was still some preparation going on, so my companion and I resumed the conversation we had been having. Though I don't recall what we were talking about, I do remember it was something really funny, so we laughed. It wasn't a little chuckle or giggle but a full-blown, toss-your-head-back laugh, where the thing seems even funnier just because you're laughing so hard. It felt good, like a really good laugh does, and we were both fully in it when we heard a loud hiss from in front of us. *"Shhhhhhhhhhhh!"* A woman in the next row was motioning at us with her eyebrows furrowed deeply and index finger mashed against her lips. Her face was contorted in something that looked like anguish. She was obviously not as amused as we felt. *"Shhhhhhhhhhh,"* she hushed us again. I'm sure we now both looked confused as to what the problem could possibly be. "We're *supposed* to be being *mindful!*" she said through clenched teeth.

While I certainly didn't consider myself an expert on mindfulness, I had a pretty good idea that being quiet was *not* what it was all about. Mindfulness seems to get misrepresented as all sorts of other things such as being pious, reverent, moving re-a-l-l-l-y s-l-l-l-o-o-o-w-w-l-y, or tiptoeing around everyone and everything. But if that's what mindfulness really required, it would be impossible to function in everyday life in the world. In my mind, if there is anything that Buddhist principles are about, it's being in your everyday life.

Very much like the idea of enlightenment, mindfulness can sometimes sound like a distant, New Age-y concept that we have to have a special quality to get to. "Oooh, how amazing, he's so mindful." But it should never be placed far away from us in that way. We can't afford to make mindfulness something special that is outside our reach, because it is so essential to our being aware. Mindfulness is the key to being fully in our lives. It's the skill that we need to cultivate in order to be present in the moment at hand. It isn't something that we can get from someplace else, but like all of the benefits of a spiritual practice, it isn't out of our reach. *All* we need to do is practice.

Right Here, Right Now

Mindfulness just means being in the moment that you're actually in. It's about really being here, being present. Not in the past. Not thinking about what you ate yesterday, what shoes you should have worn, what you *could* have done or *should* have been. We spend so much of our time in the past. Dwelling in the past persists as one of the states of mind that we habitually get stuck in. That being-stuck holds us back and keeps us from moving on. With full awareness of the present moment, we can experience our potential, rather than just looking at it from the outside.

Our personal and collective history is extremely important for understanding where we come from, what lessons we need to learn, and what mistakes we need to avoid repeating. But living in the past is useful to no one. It is pertinent that all children, black, white, Asian, and otherwise, learn about the terrible legacy of slavery that is part of our national history. It cannot ever go ignored or forgotten. At the same time, it needn't continue to be a chain that keeps us from moving forward. Acknowledging our past is necessary; living in it is a form of escape.

We don't want to get caught up in the future, either. There's nothing wrong with looking forward to events to come, but not if the looking forward is at the expense of your life right now. Living in the future is like moving through the world with your head stretched way out in front of you. Your neck would be strained and your body would become very tired. It's the same when we do this with our minds. We spend a lot of time using our energy and wearing ourselves out about things that haven't yet happened. Setting goals is important, but even our goals can be harmful when we allow them to make us become rigid and inflexible. We can be so busy worrying about where we are going that we completely miss where we are. And being anywhere other than in the present moment means we're missing our lives. When we get too stuck in the past or future, the quality of right now suffers. In fact, you miss *now* altogether. And if life doesn't happen right here, right now, when does it?

We spend a lot of time talking about how we'd much rather be someplace else, doing something else. We want to have a different life than this one. We want a different job. We want to live in a different home. In frustration, we sometimes even say that we wish we had a different life. We can make up fantastic dreams about when our lives "really" begin. How can we be so sure of what that will look like if we aren't even living the one we already have? If we want to be able to appreciate and live fully our hopes and dreams when they arrive, what better practice than to pay attention to the life we have here and now? Looking for our lives beyond right now is the very thing that causes us to miss so much of it. The result is that we are not attentive to our lives that are right in front of us. It's the not being here for each moment that makes us feel like we're out there floating, disconnected from our everyday life.

Our pursuit of material success is one of the places where we see this happen most often. Because we are busy worrying about our careers, we may forget how important it is that we spend time with our families. We can become so caught up in what we have to do to achieve success that the stuff that's really important just passes us by.

Paying Attention

I had been living completely alone in a secluded, wooded area for two years when my cousin and her three kids came to share the house I was in. Before that, I had only my two dogs and a cat to make conversation with. There's a big town about a half hour away, but I spent most of my time alone. Cindy and I are first cousins and only a few months apart in age. Starting at around age nine, we went to camp together for a few years along with my older cousin, Michelle. But because we were so close in age, it was Cindy and I that got lumped together all the time. Fortunately, we liked each other and always got along well.

By the time we got to high school, we didn't see each other nearly as much. Our lives went in different directions and we generally didn't see each other for one or two years at a time after that, but whenever we did, we were still very close. Time ran by and she had married and had three kids when we really found each other again. She was tired of the city rat race and I was finding that living alone in a big house in the center of Nowhere was not as appealing as it once had been. Also, there's a great school system where I live, along with plenty of trees and grass and other good kid things. Since I was making plans to travel more often, it made sense that she and her kids move into the house so that it wouldn't be sitting there wastefully empty.

My cousin's middle child, a bright-eyed seven-year-old girl, both loved and had a fear of one of my dogs. Legend was a very husky *and* clumsy 140-pound Rottweiler. He had a habit of running full-speed and crashing into and leaning heavily against people that he liked, and he *loved* Robbie. One afternoon, on the way out to pick up Tomeca, the oldest girl, my cousin asked me to be aware of Robbie's bus coming at 4 P.M. She could walk up the long, steep driveway alone, but Legend would definitely knock her right back down with his over-enthusiasm, so he needed to be called inside. Fine, I could handle that. I called Legend in to stay with me, and at five minutes to four, I heard the bus arrive at the bottom of the hill and make the U-turn like it always does. I was busy making plans to get my latest ideas in the works. I had to call these people tomorrow. I needed to write a letter to this person next week.

I didn't actually hear Robbie come in, but the house is large enough and I was busy enough with my own affairs that it didn't seem strange. It did occur to me for a very fleeting moment that she never came to say hello, but Robbie could be very independent when she wanted to be. In no time, I was once again too immersed in what stationery I should choose and what design to use to give Robbie much more thought. Fifteen minutes later, Cindy pulled into the driveway. I continued mulling over my future ideas and it was eight o'clock before I emerged from my office.

When I finally saw Robbie, I asked her why she didn't come to say hello when she came in. She looked confused and just shrugged. Okay, whatever. I wasn't up for pressing her. *Kids are so funny*, I thought to myself. Then Cindy turned to her and said, "Robbie, don't go down to that lady's house again." *Lady? What lady*, I wondered. "Whose house, Cindy?" It turned out that Robbie was so afraid that the dog might be loose, she decided to walk down the road to the next house rather than be rushed by Legend. Not just next-door. My seven-year-old cousin was walking down the long, snaking road that leads to the highway when her mother found her. Robbie was just about to get in a woman's car. Fortunately, the woman was a teacher and had no bad intentions. But because I hadn't engaged the matter *at all*, because I wasn't paying attention to what was important right now, Robbie ended up in a potentially dangerous situation. I was so involved in making plans and setting goals for later, I lost sight of what needed my attention in this moment. I was not being mindful or aware.

That's the way it happens. There can be warnings and signals left and right, but because we are not being alert and active, we miss or ignore them in favor of not being present. It was too hard somehow for me to stop doing what I thought was important to notice what was going on around me. Of course I felt that I knew better than this. I wanted to be angry and punish myself. But it's important to realize that none of us is perfect and we will all make mistakes. And this is exactly why we continue to practice over and over again.

Letting Go

The practice used to experience mindfulness is sometimes referred to as "letting go." Letting go means simply releasing the thoughts and ideas that our minds get in the habit of attaching themselves to, including the ideas of yesterday and tomorrow. Letting go is not hard or harsh. We should let it be easy and gradual. Our habitual way of reacting makes us feel as if we have to go on a journey with every thought that comes, or that we have to wrestle them to the ground to control them. That isn't true at all. None of our actions will be forced or contrived if we keep from grasping at everything that appears in front of us.

In meditation, we can watch how letting go works and how mindfulness develops. When we are sitting very still, counting our breaths, we focus all of our attention on the path that the breath travels through our body. We follow our breath and nothing else. Each time we notice that we have been thinking about something other than counting, we start off with 1 again. But as you are sitting there being still, you start to notice how easily your own mind just wanders off like a curious dog, sniffing at everything possible when you just want her to come on and stay close by. And just like a dog-owner, when your mind starts to pull this way and that, you give the leash a little tug at first. "Hey, where the hell are you going? We're supposed to be counting to ten and paying attention to breath." Minds and dogs are great in that you can get their attention pretty easily when you call to them—for a minute anyway. But then you start over with 1, inhale, 2, exhale, 3 . . . and off they go again.

At first, if we're feeling okay and in good spirits, we might just pull the leash lightly, give it a quick tug and keep on stepping. But after a while (and not usually too long) it gets frustrating that your mind keeps going in a different direction than you want it to. The quick tug becomes a hard yank. The brief, "come back here" becomes a long, irritated dialogue about how "you just have no discipline," "You really are getting on my nerves," and "Why can't you just do what I say?"

After that happens a few times or if we're in a not-so-good mood, it can be a much harsher, much faster process, so fast that we are not able to control ourselves. The whole thing becomes a real fight and we pull out all the stops to win. Depending on what our usual defense mechanisms are, arrogance might take over for a while. "Well, this is just stupid anyway. I can do this, I just don't feel like it."

It's a lot like when someone has an addiction to nicotine, alcohol, sex, food, or whatever they are numbing themselves with. For a long time, they pump themselves up with, "I can stop any time I want. I'm just not ready, but I have it under control. I really do it because I just don't like people telling me what to do. But I don't have a problem like those other people do."

Another thing we use is avoidance. We hide from the feeling altogether. If it's going to challenge us, make us feel what we've been pushing away or confront what we don't want to know, we come up with some way to run, get out of it. "I just don't have the time to sit here twiddling my thumbs. My time is much more valuable than that. I'm not much of a spiritual person anyway."

You don't want to force your mind into drastic change, trying to become something different, stuffing yourself into a newly created box. You just want to open the space around it so that you can expand your vision to see things just as they are. We can see the thoughts that come up in our minds the same way a mirror "sees" things. A mirror just notices. It registers whatever passes in front of it without holding on to it in any way. It just lets go. It doesn't think about it or have a long conversation about it. Since the mirror doesn't cling to the object that it is reflecting, when the object goes, so does the reflection. It's the same way with your mind. We don't hold on to the random thoughts that arise over and over again in our minds and that can take us away from the full experience of now. We want to be aware only of our breath and nothing else. The moment that we become aware that a thought has taken form, we just relax and allow it to pass. We just notice the thoughts and we return to our breath. If nothing grabs onto the thoughts as they arise, they will keep on moving on, leaving no trace that they were ever there. Let your mind be like the mirror. Clear mirror, clear mind.

Grace

Mindfulness allows us to be in each experience as it happens, rather than getting tossed back and forth. When we direct all of our attention to our breath during meditation, we cultivate a single-pointed awareness that allows us to notice clearly what is taking place. We develop a deep sense of what is important so that we are able to respond appropriately to whatever comes before us. Grace is the composure that comes naturally when your thoughts are no longer able to shift your mind away from the details of this moment. Because we don't burden ourselves with the weight of unnecessary, idle fantasies, we can be lighter. When we feel less weighed down, we can move through our lives without resistance and with greater precision. We can respond to situations with creativity rather than with fixed ideas, and can encounter each moment of our lives with ease. Buddhists may call it equanimity or forbearance. As awakening warriors, we have the confidence to hold our heads up because we know that freedom is possible.

Living with grace also means that we are able to flow naturally and with an ease of movement because we have stopped grabbing and flailing our arms out to take hold of and control everything that passes in front of us. Grace comes from a willingness to be open to exactly what is in front of you as it is. Things that used to get lost in the background suddenly become more vivid. We hear birds singing more clearly. We feel the breeze against every little hair on our necks, arms, and shoulders. We are able to feel everything without adding distracting ideas to the feeling. When we bring our minds to rest with our breath over and over again, we are returning to the current moment. We are practicing coming back to home, being in now.

Give yourself room and time to allow the benefits of your mindfulness practice to become refined and effortless. Remember that you are working with years of habitual behavior. It would be unfair to expect someone that has been walking stooped over because they have lived in a four-foot-high room for many years to suddenly stand upright just because they know where the door leading out is. It doesn't matter whether they spent their years unaware that walking tall was even a possibility or if they knew all along that all they needed was a little room. You may never have considered that you have been missing your life. Or you might have always known that your life was passing you by and have been hoping for a hint at how to get back in it. Either way, the door is the same. Once you walk through it, you have to practice to reach your full height. The same way that your body cannot be forced to stand at full attention right away, you can't expect your mind to be fully attentive right away. Forcing either one of them will only result in more pain and frustration.

This might be a funny way to see it, but eventually, your thoughts get tired of parading in front of you and not getting a rise out of you, so they just keep on stepping. And if it's clear that you're not willing to go on their journey with them, why should they even bother? Eventually, there are fewer distractions and your mind becomes clear. So the next time you find yourself thinking that you're jealous because so-and-so got more attention, the promotion, or the better grade, you can just let it go. When you learn to be more patient than your thoughts are persistent, they stop showing up and cluttering the space in your mind. When that happens, even if it is only for a few moments, there is nothing left but you. Without your thoughts there to tell you that you *are* you, there's really nothing left at all.

We don't question ourselves because without all of the reference points that our experiences give us, there is no "self" to question. Mindfulness is where you arrive when you stop trying to convince yourself, out-talk yourself, reason with yourself, and distract yourself from right now. In fact, seeing clearly is simply what happens when you stop worrying about your "self" altogether. Let everything that you have always used to reference your "self" just fall away.

10

Fearlessness: Claiming Your Warrior-Spirit

With no obstacles in the mind, no obstacles therefore no fear.
—from the Heart of Wisdom Sutra

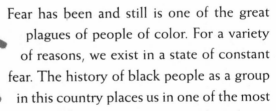 Fear has been and still is one of the great plagues of people of color. For a variety of reasons, we exist in a state of constant fear. The history of black people as a group in this country places us in one of the most unusual of circumstances: We have been here longer than almost any other non-native ethnic group, but owing to white resistance to recognize us as full human beings with the same rights as any other citizens, we have been denied much of the access that others take for granted.

Still, we are Americans. We are exposed to the same ideals about what it means to be successful, but our status as equal citizens often seems to depend on whether or not we can achieve in equal measure with our white counterparts. We battle against long-standing stereotypes. If we don't have a job, we are perceived to be lazy. If we don't get a good job, it's because we are not qualified. When we are not able to keep our jobs, regardless of the reason, it is because of our failure. We are engaged in a constant struggle to measure up. And because of the pervasive tendency in America to categorize all people by race, each one of us carries the secret burden of being a representative of our race. There is a hidden perception that if we fail to reach a goal as an individual, our entire race and community has suffered a setback.

Fear and Security

Each one of our spirits suffers from the guilt of every negative image, idea, and stereotype about black people ever conceived. And there are so many to choose from. When a news announcer says, "The rapist is described as a black man, about five foot eight inches . . ." I believe every black person that hears it feels a momentary sagging of the heart. Huge numbers of us continue to be plagued by an enormous fear of failure, and our failures somehow seem more monumental, more impossible to recover from because not only do we not have as many safety nets to catch us, but there is always the danger of systematic racism lurking nearby to keep us down as well.

It has been said many times for many years that it is the racist-minded white people that hold black people back and keep us from moving forward. In many ways that is still very true. But it is also true that we have lived so long with so much fear deep within us that we may be unable to tell if we do not move forward because we cannot or because we *will not*. The fear that lives within us is like a dirty little secret that we carry in our pockets everywhere we go. Some of us are aware of the fear and carry it inward, sheepishly struggling to keep it to ourselves. Others are less aware and direct it outward, sometimes in the form of aggression. The stereotypical angry black man isn't just angry; he is often enveloped and drowning in fear.

Fear usually comes from a perception that we are being threatened in some way. Our sense of security comes from a belief that we are in control and know what to expect. Even when the things we believe about ourselves are not positive or affirming, we feel very attached to the beliefs because they are ours.

Our security can be attacked in our minds by just about anything. We tend to feel threatened when we are in an environment that is not familiar to us. We are fearful when people that are different from us come around. We get concerned that people will take something from us, and we feel defensive. On the other hand, they may have something that we want and we feel jealous. Because of a mistaken perception that there are things outside of and separate from ourselves that we need in order to make us feel better about who we are, we feel threatened by someone else having "more" than we do. But jealousy is just the fear that we are somehow inadequate. We are lacking or not complete or not going to have enough. There is an enormous mentality of poverty that we suffer that is born out of fear.

Sometimes we have friends or lovers that have very strong personalities and we have a lot of tension with them that makes us angry. This may happen because we are not so sure of ourselves and we feel that we won't be able to preserve who we are. Instead, we believe we'll be absorbed by their strength, and we struggle against our internal fears, creating friction with the person for no real reason. Since we don't want other people to know that we are uncomfortable, we respond by going to a set of knee-jerk reactions. Our fear gets turned outward and it ends up looking like hate. We don't take the time to examine what's really going on inside us.

Fear also has a basis in desire. From very early on in our lives, we're given signals that tell us what is acceptable and what is not.

We are presented with rewards when we do the "right" thing and have what is meaningful to us withheld or taken away from us when we do not. Not only does this lock us into seeking approval in order to maintain what we feel that we need or want, it also makes what we want seem even more desirable. The "object" of our desire doesn't have to be an object at all. It could be our mother's attention, our father's affection, our teacher's approval, our friends' acceptance, or our lover's assurances that they will never leave. Right from the beginning, we are socialized to feel as if we have to act within a certain range, be limited, if we want to gain what we want and maintain what we have.

Never being afraid isn't what fearlessness is about. What fearlessness is really about is knowing that you are afraid . . . and acting anyway. When you cultivate fearlessness, you are making true bravery a part of your life. You are claiming your warrior-spirit. We call people brave when there is a dangerous situation that they are fully aware of and they still take the risk. "Aware" is the key word. Even if we accomplish great things and are considered successful by others, we can't be considered brave if we're not aware of what we are doing.

Doing It Anyway

My father has been a fireman for as long as I can remember. My grandfather was among the first black firefighters, and my father always wanted to be one. He spent his time hanging around the firehouse as a boy, and not long after I was born he become one himself. In New York City, policemen are called "The Finest," but firemen have been given the nickname "The Bravest." I always liked that my dad was one of The Bravest. I didn't realize until years later just how brave they really are.

When I was in the sixth grade, I came home to find a slew of firetrucks clustered on the corner across the street from my building. I began looking for my dad's truck right away because his firehouse was not very far from our block and I knew he should be there. The building burning was a home for kids and teenagers with special needs. There were two floors, and the house was made of brick, which my father had always told me made for a very hot fire. I'd been inside once, so I also knew there were at least ten bedrooms that the firefighters would have to look through to make sure that everyone was out. Thick, heavy smoke rolled out of the windows with an intensity that made it seem fearful and alive. I didn't see my father anywhere even though lots of the men were outside. There were still firemen connecting and dragging hoses, so they must have arrived not too long ago.

Having become a fireman at such an early age, my father was promoted to lieutenant quite young. And being lieutenant meant he was "the first to go," as he'd always told me. I couldn't see any flames, just the smoke racing out, filling the daytime sky with clouds of soot. The counselors and kids that had lived in the home were scattered everywhere with dazed looks on their faces. Some of them looked as if they'd been sleeping, standing on the grass lawn in pajamas or wrapped in blankets. We were all staring at the building in anticipation. There was some noise amongst the firemen listening to their radios, and in the next moment, out of the front door came my father, with a cloak of smoke surrounding him. He was taking his white lieutenant's helmet off as he left, walking with his head down, thick boots clunking along. When he looked up and saw me, he smiled and headed in my direction. His face was completely covered in black soot. It was as if he had a mask of greasepaint on that he smeared as he wiped at his face.

I was excited to see him and felt important because everyone could see that he was talking to me. I teased him about how dirty and stinky he was and the fact that because of the smoke, he had an embarrassing amount of mucus on his moustache. He promptly flung it off to the side explaining that it always happened. As for the building, flames were now visible in the upper windows, and the smoke was so thick that it was hard to make out the entrance any longer. The firemen were spraying water everywhere to douse the fire and I could hear the glass windows shattering. It looked very impressive and also very scary. Before we could say anything more, my father's radio screeched that there was still someone in the building. He turned and ran off faster than I could realize what was happening. At first, I thought he was going to direct the rescue effort because he was the boss on the site, but he was heading with fierce determination right back into the suffocating smoke. The flames that were licking out of almost every window were now dancing around the frame of the front door as well. Without any hesitation at all, my father stormed right back in the way he'd come out. After a few very long minutes, he came back out shaking his head. It had been a false call, there was no one else inside. To my surprise, my dad was smiling.

I've been impressed with that memory for many years. Having already been inside, my father was perfectly aware of how hot it was, that it was so smoky that he would be practically blind going in. And at that time, the firemen didn't wear masks too often, so he would also be nearly choked. But he went in anyway. Over and over again in his life, my father responds to these calls to be the first man to walk into a situation that everyone else is scrambling to get away from. He doesn't do it because he's crazy or reckless or careless about his life. He doesn't do it because he is just not afraid. He has chosen to know as much as he can about the danger involved, about what makes the situation as scary as it seems to someone like you and me. Armed with that awareness, he acts with warrior-spirit and does it anyway.

Facing Our Fears

When we are young and discover the idea of friendly, we run around and hug *everyone*. When we discover kissing, we walk up and kiss other children whether they are boys or girls, black, white, or Asian. As a child, it wasn't that you were taking a risk, it was more that you were acting spontaneously and without fear. That kissing, hugging child you once were connected with a feeling that came directly from the heart. You showed affection without a sense of restriction. That kind of action, coming directly from the heart, is missing from our adult lives.

It was not so much that you didn't know any better, it was that you were not yet self-conscious. You weren't so conscious of your "self" that you felt you had to erect walls of suspicion, hesitation, and resistance around yourself. But as you grow older, you begin to construct more ideas about exactly who your "self" is. It's only the activity of your mind and the sensations of your body that keep you separated, that draw the line between "me" here and "you" over there. But Me and You are only ideas that we have made to describe what we see as the difference between us. The moment that we do that, the potential for conflict begins. When there isn't a "me" that stands separate and apart from "you," there's no need to feel threatened, so there's no need to feel fear.

We make a big deal about the idea of self-preservation, but I think we start getting the hang of it very early. We attach ourselves to a fixed idea of a self that needs to be preserved. Then we wonder why we are unable to move beyond those fixed ideas. How can we expect to act fully and completely from our hearts if we have placed so many limitations on ourselves in our minds? The less of a defined and rigid sense of self we have, the less likely we are to feel as if we have to protect that self. We don't so much need to be taught how to preserve the self as much as we do how to release the self.

A practice of meditation can provide us with a safe space in which to sit face-to-face with our fears. It allows us to take the time to feel what it is we are afraid of and explore where those fears come from. When we really begin to examine all the different aspects of ourselves, our tendency is to run and hide or to become resistant and try to ignore what we know in our hearts to be true. It is the turning away and the resistance that keeps us stuck in a place of fear. It's definitely a frustrating experience and can even be devastating for some of us. It's not that we are bad or hopeless people that don't know how to handle anything. What we have been taught in life is to close up and become defensive when something is not familiar or expected or within our control. When things become difficult for us to face, we do everything we can to turn away. We don't want to experience pain. When feelings or situations are unfamiliar, our sense of who we are is somehow threatened and we poise ourselves for battle. We pull from deeper and deeper layers of built-up fear, anxiety, and insecurity.

But with practice, by returning over and over again to face what is there with curiosity and gentleness, we can begin to see the things that hold us back—and the way to walk right through them. Facing a problem head-on and stepping right through it rather than being evasive and hiding from it in the hopes that it'll go away is what is meant by transcending. Transcending something doesn't make it go away, it just means that you get on the other side of it. You get on the side that doesn't let the fear keep you from moving forward anyway. Making a practice of becoming comfortable enough with our fears that we don't get stuck in one place or turn and run in the other direction helps us to act in accord with the warrior-spirit that is our original nature.

Acting in tune with our original nature means that we are not restricted by all of the buildup of information. There's no hesitation in our actions because we don't reference our long history of experience. When we train this area, we bypass every single piece of information that told us we couldn't say or do this or that, that we weren't good enough. Not only is it a fear of failure that holds us back; if we have long believed the myth that we are not good enough, we can even become frozen by a fear of our success. There is a place that we find when we look deeply into ourselves that allows us to be completely free of our histories, our stories, our hang-ups. Once we realize that we cannot really control the outcome, we can let go of the procrastination that comes from being fearful of the results. We can stop letting desire for the approval of someone else make us hesitant. We don't have to live in the shadow of anyone's expectations of us. Not those of white America, nor those of our parents or lovers. Instead, we can all live our lives for the sake of the experience itself because we come to realize that is what we have. The experience of life, the actual doing it, living it, is what we have to savor. We actually have a freedom spot in our brains!

Joy and Pain

Fearlessness is going to meet ourselves, going to meet our pain and letting go of our fear so that we can move with ease. But it is *also* releasing our tight grip on joy so we can fully experience it as it is, undistorted by our desire to make it stay. Practice brings us home to ourselves again and again, in the face of fear, in the face of pain, so that we can remain connected to our lives in each moment. When the storm winds blow, when the baby cries, when we want to turn and run away, fearlessness keeps us present and alive.

Cultivating fearlessness gives us the capacity to kick the door to our lives wide open and feel empowered to walk through. When we no longer let fear get in the way of action, we move through life without hesitation. Everything we do is more decisive because we are aware of where we are. We are more determined because we have already opened our eyes to the situation and made the decision to move forward, starting from a place of understanding. Without a real or imagined expectation of danger, our actions can become bold and direct. Claiming our warrior-spirits means that we assume a position of responsibility for our lives. We commit to being active and not just idly waiting for suffering to end. We acknowledge our confusion, aggression, anger, pain, passion, and the chaos in the world, and we pursue life with all our might anyway.

11

Wake Up: A Call for Transformation

Black people are natural, they possess the secret of joy. . . . They are alive physically and emotionally, which makes them easy to live with.

—Mirella Ricciardi, African Saga, 1982
from *Possessing the Secret of Joy* by Alice Walker

明 I fully believe this to be true.

How powerful it would be if we all, blacks and non-blacks alike, recognized this truth, even if only for an instant? What if we as black folks were to make a practice of touching such a reality every day? A radical transformation would begin.

What we imagine ourselves to be looking for as black Americans is not out there. It is in here, in our hearts. What we need in order to be equal as people of color in a country that often divides us on the basis of the color of our skin is to be found not in further separation, greater division, but in oneness and intimacy. It is the separation from our true selves that keeps us from enjoying personal happiness, just as it is the separation of races that divides us from the promise of an America that can begin to meet our hopes and dreams.

Contrary to popular belief, the prevailing religion of America isn't Christianity, it's Individual Materialism. It's a system that endorses blind self-interest and urges us to look away from the suffering of everyone around us in favor of our own financial and material gain. If we all take this position, it will never work out because the world is getting smaller and smaller.

Our ability to reach the other side of the country, the continent, or indeed, the planet is incredibly accessible. We can see clearly how our words and actions can now touch people across what once seemed like impossible boundaries in an instant. Technology and science have brought us all closer together while our prevailing system of thinking/functioning works to create distance between us in our hearts and spirits.

The work to create laws against racism is indeed necessary, but we cannot rely on such laws alone. They are just reminders that we need to recondition ourselves. We must take responsibility for our collective reconditioning with regard to discrimination, but even more important, with regard to our own self-acceptance, awareness, and healing.

The things that will destroy us are: politics without principle; pleasure without conscience; wealth without work; knowledge without character; business without morality; science without humanity, and worship without sacrifice.

—Mahatma Gandhi

It is not the responsibility of our government to tend to the spirit. It is not even the responsibility of our spiritual guides. It is the responsibility of you and me. Politics, government, even democracy will always fail in this area because those ideas all respond to numbers. Spiritual practice responds to our individual consciences, our morality, our hearts and spirits.

In order to take on that responsibility, we have to wake up to each minute of every day and take full responsibility for the changes that we want to make in our lives and in our world. But we can't do that effectively if we haven't yet made peace with our own selves. We can take up no battles—philosophical, social or otherwise—without first transcending the stories we make up in our own minds about ourselves and our shortcomings, and also the stories of others. It's the labels that we apply and that are applied to us that box us in, break us down, and wear us out. Contrary to popular belief, the way to transformation in our lives is not to put on a heavy coat of armor and carry a thick shield, it's to put those things down. We have to be willing to expose our most tender areas and commit to setting aside anything and everything that puts a barrier between us and the world. That's the only way in which to allow our love and compassion to take their natural place as the source of action.

The walls that we build around ourselves both mentally and physically give us the dangerous false illusion that we are safe, but there's no such thing as a wall that cannot be torn down. When we invest ourselves in the idea that we have erected this wall for protection, we naturally make enemies of anything on the other side of the wall. We close ourselves in further and further, creating more and more distance not only between black folks and white folks, the African Diaspora and Latinos. We also create distance between us and our mothers, children, lovers, and most of all, ourselves.

Practicing Buddhists have a task to engage in as well. America's unique stamp on and responsibility to Buddhism lies in this culture's capacity to formulate a practice of Dharma that transcends boundaries of race, class, gender, and sexuality. One of the things that all human beings fiercely cling to is "sameness." Our individual identities are falsely wrapped up in and reinforced by relations to people that are "the same" as us. We have been taught to resist difference, to resist change. Buddhism teaches us that resistance to positive change comes from our habits and patterns. But never has Buddhism been practiced in such a widely diverse culture. We have the rare opportunity to actualize a *Buddhadharma* that truly incorporates diversity and recognizes our basic equality. This seems to me to be the most fundamental message of the Buddha's teaching. No separation. No difference. We are all One. Surely, we cannot spend so much time looking into ourselves and not just see, but act upon the classism and racism that lives there. Those illusions perpetuate themselves within our expression of the Buddhadharma. If we are to truly adhere to the warrior-spirit of the Bodhisattva ideal as Americans practicing Dharma, we must make it our highest priority to make the effort to invite more people of color into the Sanghas of practitioners. We have to make welcome everyone that wants to walk in the footsteps of the Buddha. We have to accept this challenge actively and resist making the Buddha's teachings special, accessible only to a privileged few, under the guise of "saving it" from secularization. Anything short of a full-blown revolution is willful ignorance and a display of an elitist egotism at its worst.

What we all need is to learn to live without walls. We have to let the illusion of separation fall away and replace it with active, lively engagement of every aspect of our lives. This is not just for personal growth, but collective growth. This is not intended as self-help, but self-examination. It's taking a long, piercing gaze at who you are in the world, who you perceive your "self" to be, and then transcending all those ideas so that you can live freely, un-fixated, unselfish, and clear. In other words, it's not about working on yourself but waking yourself up.

One way to slow down and begin to change our perspective is to begin to measure our lives by each breath we take, rather than by each day, month, or year. Meditation invites us to do that. It's not meditation that changes you. Meditation just wakes you up to things as they are. It won't make a better you or a worse you. But it will reveal you. When we become aware of ourselves, we find the potential for radical transformation. If you want to change, that's where you have to start from. If you really wake up, if you really notice, it's inevitable that change will take place. When all is said and done, introspection and your spiritual practice will take you exactly back where you started from. The path that you follow is not about going somewhere, but about coming back to you. Over and over again. Only this time, you are awake to who that is and the life that you are living. You end up seeing that, without reservation, everything you need you already have. And anything you think you don't have, you don't need anyway.

We are still entirely different people with many different needs. Our unique cultures, geographies, and histories shape the way in which we develop our organizations and systems of being in the world. But we do not all need to believe in the same God to live without fear, gracefully and in peace with one another. What we can agree on is compassion. We don't have to express it in the exact same way, but we must all agree to practice and live with compassion for others in our hearts. What we have to agree on is that we will continue to do our best to transform.

Accessing the skills we need to master life isn't instant, and I can't promise you that they will be easy for you to get to. I can promise that no matter who you are or where you come from, they are there and they are available to you and always will be. With time, patience, and the spirit of desire to realize your own truth, you'll find them just where they've been all along. Inside you.

12

Suggestions for Further Study: Pointing the Way

Vast is the robe of liberation
A formless field of benefaction
I wear the Buddha's teaching
Saving all sentient beings
—**Verse of the Buddha's Robe**

As we step onto a path of change, it is helpful to take a moment to consider how blessed we are to have the gift of other people's experiences to share. So much of what we come to explore in our lives is a result of having the opportunity to receive the insight of others who have experienced pain or gained insights and have had the courage and grace to share what they have learned with the rest of us. I've learned from many, many books and subtle teachers along the way. I have gained the most from people with a vision of peaceful living in the world, who have backed up their vision with demanding action.

People as Role Models

Among the mentors I have never known are Mahatma Gandhi, Martin Luther King, Jr., Dr. B. R. Ambedkar, Malcolm X, His Holiness the XIV Dalai Lama, Jane Addams, Thomas Merton, and Dorothy Day.

Books

In areas related to exploring my spirituality and who I am in the world, certain books began to point the way:

Zen

Though D. T. Suzuki's *Zen and Japanese Culture* was the first book I encountered about Zen, it wasn't really my introduction to the practice of the Zen school of Buddhism that I have come to deeply love and appreciate. *Zen Mind, Beginner's Mind*, by Shunryu Suzuki, remains my personal bible and the book that I myself return to and recommend to others over and over again. It's a classic written by a Japanese priest who was largely responsible for planting one of the most fertile seeds of Zen in Western soil. By the time he passed away, Suzuki Roshi had sufficiently transplanted Zen to a small temple on Page Street in San Francisco that has since grown into one of the most respected and prolific Zen centers in the country. It made sense that, having fallen in love with Zen via Suzuki Roshi's book, I should take my first meditation instruction at the San Francisco Zen Center while visiting the West Coast. I still get their newsletter and make a point of going there anytime I end up on that side of the country.

While *The Three Pillars of Zen*, by Phillip Kapleau, isn't for the casual seeker, it comes complete with a basic history and explanations of many Japanese terms and rituals. Kapleau—who eventually became a Roshi and nurtured the Rochester Zen Center, in New York State, into a vibrant community before retiring—establishes that there are three things that are essential to Zen: (1) great faith, (2) great doubt, and (3) great determination. Whether by accident or on purpose, Kapleau has defined Zen practice very simply as what we all need in order to make a practice of engaging our lives fully.

Being Black

Because of the vast diversity of our experience as black people, it would be impossible to say there is any book, contemporary or otherwise, that gives a full picture of what the black experience is all about. What *Breaking Bread: Insurgent Black Intellectual Life*, coauthored by Cornel West and bell hooks, does, though, is offer a glimpse at a wide range of experience, cause and effect of black life in America from the perspective of two of our most respected intellectuals. Almost ten years later, the book is as relevant and insightful as ever. It has enough references throughout the text and in the selected bibliography to offer any reader a knowledge base for better understanding the history of love, work, and play that makes up being black in America.

The Black Notebooks, by Toi Derricote, chronicles an experience completely foreign to almost every American: that of a person who has been seen and accepted as both black and white at different moments in time. Derricote's journals reveal the conflict and pain of living in a society in which white skin privilege garners instant access and black blood awareness garners rejection from everyone around.

Spirituality

Chogyam Trungpa Rinpoche's classic book, *Cutting Through Spiritual Materialism*, continues to be a standard reference for the most basic ideals of pursuing a spiritual path without letting the idea of pursuing it take over as the most important thing. Trungpa Rinpoche, like Suzuki Roshi with Zen, tirelessly presented and refined the practice of Tibetan Buddhism to appeal to the Western mind. He went even further by establishing a secular system of spiritual training called Shambhala Training, basing it on the noble ideals of the lost Shambhala Warriors. His small book, *Shambhala: The Sacred Path of the Warrior*, is an inspiring glimpse into the possibilities that basic goodness can bring.

And when crisis becomes a part of our lives, as it inevitably does, *When Things Fall Apart: Heart Advice for Difficult Times*, by Pema Chodron, is a great book to have nearby to simply remind ourselves that the best we can do is our best and that is just fine. It has taught me that when things begin to fall apart, instead of hiding from the experience, I can try to accept it as an opportunity to reexamine and appreciate all the pieces of my life that make up the whole. Chodron was Trungpa Rinpoche's student and is now an American Buddhist teacher with her own following. Her book speaks in the direct, plain, loving language we all need to hear when we have forgotten that we are not alone and that the response we must have to the pain in our lives is not to close down but to open our hearts wider to love.

Love

Unfortunately, there are not enough books written about love itself. There are magazine articles and television shows about how to get love, find love, keep it, and wrestle it to the ground, but not much at all about the nature of love and what part it plays in our lives. bell hooks's *All About Love* is a book that anyone who has even had a question about love can read and learn from.

Additional Books

Some other resources that I have learned from and appreciated for their insights into different areas are:

COMMUNITY SERVICE

Compassion in Action, by Ram Dass and Mirabai Bush

LEADERSHIP

I May Not Get There with You, by Michael Eric Dyson

MEDITATION

The Wooden Bowl, by Clark Strand

PEACEMAKING

Bearing Witness, by Roshi Bernie Glassman

RACE AND DIVERSITY IN BUDDHISM

Making the Invisible Visible<Healing Racism in Our Buddhist Communities. Booklet presented to Conference on Buddhist Teachers in the West, June 2000. (Available as e-book at www.edharma. com)

"Asian American Buddhist Communities," in *Turning Wheel: Quarterly Journal of the Buddhist Peace Fellowship,* Fall 2000.

Rick Fields, "Confessions of a White Buddhist," in *Tricycle: The Buddhist Review*, Fall 1994: 54–56.

Zoketsu Norman Fischer, "On Difference and Dharma," in *Tricycle: The Buddhist Review*, Summer 1999: 19.

Addie Foye, "Buddhists in America: A Short, Biased View," in *Tricycle: The Buddhist Review* Fall 1994: 57.

bell hooks, "Contemplation and Transformation," in Marianne Dresser, ed., *Buddhist Women on the Edge* (Berkeley: North Atlantic Books, 1996), pp. 287–92.

bell hooks, "Waking Up to Racism," in *Tricycle: The Buddhist Review*, Fall 1994: 42–45.

Victor Sogen Hori, "Sweet-and-Sour Buddhism," in *Tricycle: The Buddhist Review*, Fall 1994: 48–52.

Charles Johnson, "A Sangha by Another Name," in *Tricycle: The Buddhist Review*, Winter 1999: 43–47, 110–12.

Russell Leong, "Litany," in *Tricycle: The Buddhist Review*, Fall 1994: 58–63.

Jan Nattier, "Visible and Invisible: Jan Nattier on the Politics of Representation in Buddhist America," in *Tricycle: The Buddhist Review*, Fall 1995: 42–49.

Joe Parker, "The Cost of Buddhist Practice: Class, Access and Diversity," in *Turning Wheel: Journal of the Buddhist Peace Fellowship*, Spring 2000: 33–35.

Lori Pierce, "Outside In: Buddhism in America," in Marianne Dresser, ed., *Buddhist Women on the Edge* (Berkeley: North Atlantic Books, 1996), pp. 93–104.

Charles S. Prebish and Kenneth K. Tanaka, eds., *The Faces of Buddhism in America* (Berkeley: University of California Press, 1998).

RACE AND PEOPLE OF COLOR IN AMERICA

Autobiography of Malcolm X, by Malcolm X and Alex Haley
Black Feminist Thought, by Patricia Hill Collins

Black Looks: Race and Representation, by bell hooks
Invisible Man, by Ralph Ellison
Killing Rage: Ending Racism, by bell hooks
Off White: Readings on Race, Power and Society, by Michelle Fine
A People's History of the United States, by Howard Zinn
Playing in the Dark: Whiteness and the Literary Imagination, by Toni Morrison
Race Matters, by Cornel West

Organizations

Order of Interbeing
   Meditation groups founded by Vietnamese Zen monk Thich Nhat Hahn.
http:///www.parallax.org

Peacemaker Community
   An international network of clergy and laypeople dedicated to facilitating peacemaking as a way of life.
2022 Cliff Drive, #276
Santa Barbara, CA 93109
805-565-7566
http://www.peacemakercommunity.org

Shammbhala International
   A worldwide network of meditation centers, founded by Chogyam Trungpa Rinpoche, a master of the Shambhala and Tibetan Buddhist traditions.
Karme-Choling Center
369 Patneaude Lane
Barnet, Vermont 05821
http://www.shambhala.org

Urban Peace Project and Foundation
Urban Peace, Inc.
P.O. Box 563
Spencer, NY 14883-0563

National virtual membership organization using technology and popular culture to support and facilitate peacemaking in urban communities. Uses corporate, for-profit models and affinity relationships to redirect wealth to existing nonprofits, empowering them to compete for visibility and funding. Strategies include training clergy and laypeople to enter a formal practice of peacemaking and continuous learning, including communication, problem-solving, counseling, and so on.
http://www.urbanpeace.com
info@urbanpeace.com

Web Sites

beingblack.com—official Web site for *Being Black,* with tour schedule, information updates, forum for exploration of black identity and spirituality.

buddhanet.net—Buddhist Information Network, with emphasis on Theravada information.

buddhismandracism.org—"Healing Racism in Our Sanghas" meetings are gatherings primarily for European Americans from all Buddhist traditions. Web site with bulletin board.

dharmaplanet.com—Eastern spirituality–based community site with guest chat, radio shows, bulletin boards, calendar of events, etc.

dharmanet.org—large online database-drive Web site of information and contacts.

edharma.com—online magazine featuring articles, book reviews with emphasis on the culture of Dharma in America and on diversity, race, relationships, and practice.

egroups.com/group/blackbuddhists—online disucssion group provides a means by which black Buddhists as well as Christians, Muslims, and others can come together and explore the ways in which Buddhist teachings and meditation can illuminate our spiritual journeys and help us to lead more satisfying, meaningful, and skillful lives. Free online mailing list.

rainbowdharma.com—a loosely organized group of Buddhist people of color on the Internet. Web site with bulletin board.

gaybuddhist.org—Gay Buddhist Fellowship.

Magazines and Publications

Here are various publications that can be explored. They are listed in order of the most general to the more specific.

Shambhala magazine

Tricycle: The Buddhist Review

What Is Enlightenment

FPMT—Foundation for the Preservation of the Mahayana Tradition

AN EXPLANATION OF THE CHARACTERS

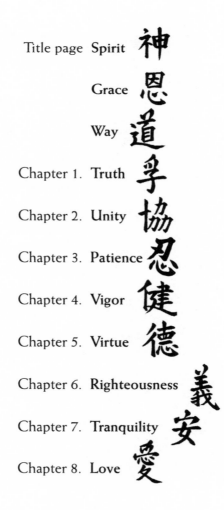

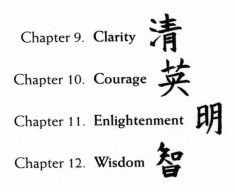

INDEX

Page numbers in *italics* refer to illustrations.